Plant Pruning
A to Z

Plant Pruning
A to Z

Jon Muller

David & Charles

A DAVID & CHARLES BOOK

David & Charles is a subsidiary of F+W (UK) Ltd.,
an F+W Publications Inc. company

First published in the UK by David & Charles Ltd in 2004
First published in New Zealand by David Bateman Ltd in 2004

ISBN 0 7153 1924 8

Printed in China by Everbest Printing Company
for David & Charles
Brunel House   Newton Abbot   Devon

Visit our website at www.davidandcharles.co.uk

David & Charles books are available from all good bookshops; alternatively you can
contact our Orderline on (0)1626 334555 or write to us at FREEPOST EX2110, David &
Charles Direct, Newton Abbot, TQ12 4ZZ (no stamp required UK mainland).

Acknowledgements

I would like to thank David Palmer, my technical editor, whose patient attention to detail was
much appreciated. For practical help and advice, Dave Aitchison from Arbortech and Martin
Herbert from Waikato Polytechnic were very helpful. Andrew Ladley of Victoria University
helped to demystify the law with regard to trees.

Photographic Credits

All photographs supplied by GEOFF BRYANT, except for:
GLOBAL BOOK PUBLISHING PHOTO LIBRARY: *Fremontodendron mexicanum*; *Halesia carolina*; *Kunzea
parvifolia*; *Persea americana*; *Prunus armeniaca*; *Prunus cerasifera* 'Pissardii'; *Prunus persica*
'Texstar'; *Psidium guajava*; *Rubus idaeus* 'Heritage'; *Stachyurus praecox*; *Telopea speciosissima*
'Flaming Beacon'; *Umbellularia californica*.
NATURAL SCIENCES IMAGE LIBRARY OF NEW ZEALAND: (G.R. 'Dick' Roberts) coppiced basket
willow p.16; beech hedge p.24; dwarf apple trees p.27; newly staked tree p.28; *Buddleja
davidii*; *Callistemon citrinus*; *Hoheria populnea*; *Parthenocissus tricuspidata*; *Prunus* x *domestica*.

Page 1: *Hamamelis* x *intermedia*; Page 2: *Prunus subhirtella*; Page 3: *Citrus* x *meyeri*; Page 4:
Cotinus coggygria 'Purpureus'; Page 5: *Rhododendron* 'Kaponga'; Page 6: *Quercus palustris*,
with the leaves of *Fagus sylvatica* 'Purpurea' in the foreground.

Contents

Introduction

This book is designed to be a guide for students and keen gardeners wanting to prune with more understanding and skill.

Most of you have pruned your plants at some time. After looking at the pile of prunings at your feet you may well have asked, "Have I done the right thing?"

This book addresses this and other questions related to the art of pruning. It looks at the pruning and care of about 220 common plants in a simple, practical way.

Pruning is just one part of the whole picture when caring for plants. Choosing the optimum growing conditions for each plant is essential. Too often remedial pruning or removal is the result of a plant being in the wrong place to start with.

Erythrina crista-galli, with its eye-catching red flowers.

For example, planting a large tree under a power line or very close to a building is giving the tree its death warrant at a later stage. Similarly, if you plant a sun-loving plant in the shade it will tend to become leggy and flower poorly as it tries to make the most of the less than ideal conditions.

Plants are living organisms that interact with their environment constantly. They have evolved over millions of years, adapting and surviving. As humans we have changed the environment considerably, with little thought to its effects. In addition, all too often plants, especially large trees, are placed in situations where their survival is jeopardized because we have lacked understanding of their needs.

Too often trees are pruned with no understanding of the way they grow and naturally respond to damage. Arboriculture (from the word *arbor* or tree) is now taught throughout the world. The practices and principles of arboriculture clarify how to prune trees correctly. The basic practices and terms used are mentioned in this book.

Hardiness Zone Map

This map has been prepared to agree with a system of plant hardiness zones that have been accepted as an international standard and range from 1 to 12. It shows the minimum winter temperatures that can be expected on average in different regions.

In this book, where a zone number has been given, the number corresponds with a zone shown here. That number indicates the coldest areas in which the particular plant is likely to survive through an average winter.

Note that these are not necessarily the areas in which it will grow best. Because the zone number refers to the minimum temperatures, a plant given zone 7, for example, will obviously grow perfectly well in zone 8, but not in zone 6. Plants grown in a zone considerably higher than the zone with the minimum winter temperature in which they will survive might well grow but they are likely to behave differently. Note also that some readers may find the numbers a little conservative; we felt it best to err on the side of caution.

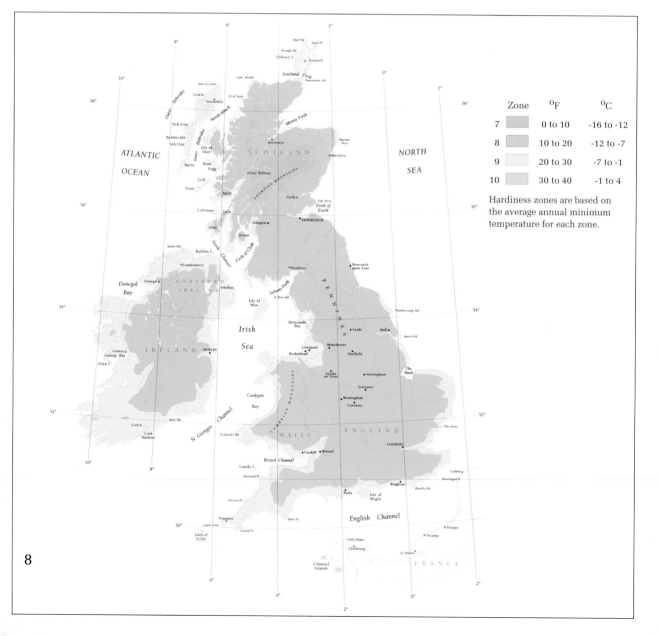

Zone		°F	°C
7		0 to 10	-16 to -12
8		10 to 20	-12 to -7
9		20 to 30	-7 to -1
10		30 to 40	-1 to 4

Hardiness zones are based on the average annual minimum temperature for each zone.

PART ONE

PLANT PRUNING

1

Principles of pruning and training

With good planning and pruning to remove the 3 Ds, your trees should be low maintenance assets in your graden. Shown here is *Ailanthus altissima* in spring. (For a summer view of this same tree see page 40.)

Pruning is the removal of any part of a plant to encourage it to grow, flower and fruit as wanted. Training is the modification of plant shape or form. Before you train or prune any plant you need to ask whether you should do anything at all.

In a forest, trees will grow closer together, resulting in dead branches at the base of the tree where there is less light. They will then naturally prune or shed dead branches. Plants naturally train their growth to maximize the light conditions. Where there are low light conditions they will tend to have leggy, spindly growth, as they extend their growth upwards.

Most trees and shrubs will also respond to prolonged wind exposure during periods of growth by growing on the side sheltered from the prevailing wind. This wind-shear effect leads to lopsided-looking growth, but is a natural response to the plant's environment. Strong winds, as well as distorting the growth of trees and shrubs, can effectively cut off growth above a certain height.

In an ornamental garden or a park you can allow trees and shrubs that naturally grow close together more space to expand and can train them for optimum shape and health.

As a general principle you need to consider the overall effect of removing growth from a plant in terms of its ability to grow, reproduce and maintain and repair itself. As a rule of thumb, do not remove more than a third of the growth from a plant at any one time. Removing more than this can affect the ability of the plant to carry out its functions, such as growing or reproducing. While some plants can tolerate harder pruning and still regenerate, for others severe pruning can result in death.

Before you start to prune any plants you need to ask why you are doing it, so that you get the desired result.

Reasons for pruning and training

To remove the 3 Ds: dead, damaged and diseased wood

If you only ever prune for this reason, you will have improved the health of the tree enormously. This is because not only are dead branches and stubs unsightly and dangerous, but deadwood can be a source of infection. In addition, removing deadwood will let more light into the tree, encouraging new growth. If you are unsure whether a branch is alive or dead, especially if it is a deciduous species, scratch the bark. If it is green underneath, it is alive; if brown, it is dead. Damaged wood or trees that are unstable should be removed for safety reasons. In colder climates damage can occur due to frost causing dieback or snow breaking branches.

To encourage flowering and fruiting

This may involve thinning out growth to let more light in, or cutting the plant back after flowering to encourage denser growth and better flowering. The effects of pruning on flowering are discussed below.

To improve the shape and size of trees and shrubs

This can improve light penetration, views or access around the plant.

Pieris japonica does double duty in the garden with both beautiful new red foliage and dainty white flower-bells in early spring.

Effects of pruning and training

Managing growth

If you remove the growing tips of a plant, you actually stimulate growth. This is because the apical or terminal bud at the tip of the shoot produces a hormone which inhibits the growth of the lower buds. Once this bud is removed, the lower buds develop. (See figure 1.) You can use this to good advantage when training a hedge, as regular clipping results in dense growth.

If we cut a mature branch back hard, it sometimes results in a mass of dense, spindly growth from epicormic shoots. These shoots are produced from dormant buds within the bark or stems of a tree, and often occur as a stress response to severe overpruning or storm damage. This growth is poorly attached to the tree and prone to later wind damage. When cutting back branches to reduce the size of a tree or shrub you need to prune to a node, as shown in figure 2. The node is the part of the plant where a new shoot will arise from a bud.

Slope the cut away from the direction of growth of the shoot to allow water to run away from the bud. This reduces the chance of water sitting in the bud and causing rot. Cutting the stem too far away from the bud can cause dieback, while cutting too close can cause damage to the bud.

Variegated trees or shrubs have a tendency to revert to the unvariegated form, which is more vigorous. By removing this growth whenever it occurs, you can maintain the variegated habit.

With plants that are budded or grafted the rootstock growth can take over because the rootstock is more vigorous. This growth will arise from below the graft union. It is best removed with a sharp knife or pruning shears (secateurs) as soon as it develops.

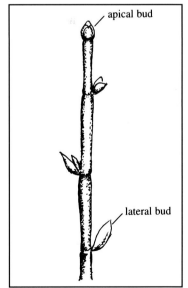

Fig. 1. Apical and lateral buds. If the apical bud is removed, the lower lateral buds develop.

11

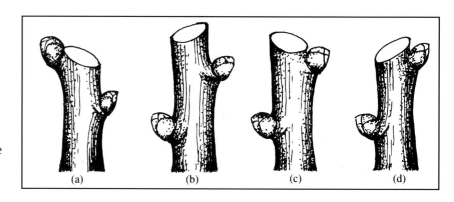

Fig. 2. Pruning to a node: cut (a) is too close to the node; cut (b) is too far away; cut (c) slopes the wrong way; cut (d) is correct.

(a)   (b)   (c)   (d)

Encouraging flowering

The effects of pruning can vary, depending on the type of growth that the plants flower on. For example, roses flower on new growth. Hard pruning encourages new growth and therefore flowering. If you don't prune roses back hard you can get spindly growth with fewer flowers.

Apples, on the other hand, flower on two-year-old and older growth. Hard pruning will encourage new growth to the detriment of flowering growth. The new growth will take two years before it starts producing fruiting wood. In this instance, apart from removing the 3 Ds (dead, damaged and diseased wood) and creating a strong framework, apples need very little pruning. (See the section on fruit tree pruning.)

The angle of a shoot influences fruiting. The more horizontal the shoot the greater the fruitfulness and less the vigor. This fact can be used to advantage when training fruit trees. You can tie down branches of fruit trees that are upright to a horizontal position to encourage fruiting or use the espalier method. (See the section on fruit trees.)

Many trees do not require pruning, other than removal of the 3 Ds, if they are planted in the right location. However, fruiting plants and flowering shrubs generally require more pruning and training.

Kunzea parvifolia benefits from pruning back after flowering to encourage more blooms next season.

2
Pruning techniques for trees

Trees generally have a well-defined woody trunk, although some large trees have many trunks. Branches arise from the trunk, with lateral branches arising from these branches. Where the trunk and branch meet there is raised bark called the branch bark ridge. This line of raised bark is an important indicator of where the final cut should be made when removing a branch, as shown in figure 3. The crown is the part of the tree containing branches and leaves, and any part of the trunk from which branches arise. There are a number of options when pruning trees.

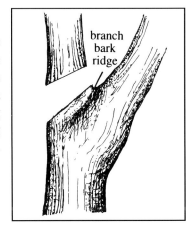

Fig. 3. Branch bark ridge. The bark ridge shown here indicates where the final cut should be made.

Crown-cleaning

This is the removal of the 3 Ds. It is an essential part of any pruning, as discussed in the section on reasons for pruning.

Crown-lifting

This involves the removal of lower branches to give better clearance under the tree. It may be done, for example, to let more light through to a house or other plants.

Crown-thinning

Crown-thinning is the removal of some growth to open up the tree without altering the size and shape of the tree. After removing the 3 Ds, remove weaker, spindly growth as well as criss-crossing branches.

Correct crown-thinning will expose the form of the tree and allow more light into the remaining branches, allowing further growth to go into the preferred form of the tree.

Fig. 4a. Crown-lifting.

Fig. 4b. Crown-thinning.

13

Fig. 4c. Crown-reduction.

Crown-reduction

Crown-reduction involves reducing the height and spread of a tree. This may be in order to clear power lines or buildings, or to improve views.

Some large trees cannot be crown-reduced, once they are mature, without damaging the tree. For example, reducing a large gum tree to improve views by cutting back the large trunks results in dieback or a mass of epicormic shoots. This compromises the health of the tree and results in denser growth, which will make the matter worse if a better view is the desired outcome.

In this case, crown-thinning and crown-raising would be a better option.

Other trees can be successfully crown-reduced. For example, magnolias can be cut back to a suitable lateral branch that is healthy and growing the correct way.

If a tree needs regular crown-reduction, it may be too large for the area. Replace it with a more suitable plant. The individual requirements for each plant are covered in Part Two, commencing on page 35.

Topping

Topping or lopping is a damaging and unsuitable technique for tree management. By indiscriminately cutting across a tree its appearance is spoilt; the resulting regrowth, if it occurs, is weak and poorly attached so that disease or structural failure often results. Avoid contractors who top trees!

Pollarding

Pollarding involves cutting back a tree during its dormant winter period to about 6 ft. (2 m) above ground level to encourage lateral rather than vertical growth. Historically, it was a method of tree management that created new wood growth which could then be used for various purposes, such as fencing. Willows were often pollarded to generate new thin branches for weaving.

Pollarding also became popular in urban areas as a means of restricting the height of a street tree, often leading to unattractive results. The London plane tree was commonly managed in this way. Luckily, this technique is not practiced as much as it used to be and it is not as damaging as topping, as trees are pruned back to a well-defined part rather than being cut indiscriminately.

Opposite: *Salix caprea* 'Pendula'

Pleaching

Pleaching is the weaving together of tree branches to form living archways, screens or hedges, where the lower trunks are bare to a height of 6–8 ft. (1.8–2.4 m) above the ground. Traditionally, pleaching involved grafting branches from separate trees together. The most suitable subjects are trees with pliable branches, such as linden trees, hawthorns and pear trees. However, it is possible to create a pleached look without the cutting and grafting. Plant your chosen trees or shrubs as you would for a hedge and train each to a single stem. Keep the lower trunk free of branches and prune the tops to encourage lateral growth. Soon a dense network of small branches and foliage will create a 'pleached' hedge. You can then prune to the shape you desire, or try topiary (see below). Choose trees with attractive trunks and dense foliage.

Coppicing

Coppicing is essentially pollarding (see above) at ground level. During the dormant winter months, branches are cut back to just above ground level, leaving a stump from which fresh shoots can grow. It is a traditional method of creating wood to harvest. Most trees can be coppiced for wood production or for ornamental purposes. For example, *Salix* species are often coppiced to produce whippy new growth used in basket weaving. It is also used to promote colorful foliage from plants such as *Cornus* species, or large attractive leaves in trees such as *Ailanthus* and *Catalpa*.

Branch removal

When large branches need to be removed, you need to know how to do this safely and correctly.

When you are obliged to climb a tree to prune you need safety climbing

A coppiced basket willow being harvested for suitable branches.

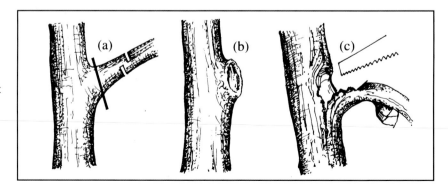

Fig. 5. Branch removal: (a) correct sequence of cuts; (b) correctly cut branch showing sealing of wound; (c) incorrect cut without undercutting, causing tearing of the bark.

gear. Removing large branches or felling trees can be dangerous to people as well as property. Large branches overhanging buildings or roads need to be lowered with ropes and safe working areas established. Use professionals for this work.

If you cut a branch using one top cut, the weight of the branch can cause the bark to tear, resulting in damage to the trunk tissue. This damage can be an entry point for disease. The correct procedure, as shown in figure 5, involves three cuts:

1. The first cut underneath the branch, cutting one-third to halfway through the branch.
2. The second cut on the upper side, a few centimeters further out from the first cut. The branch will then fall without tearing the bark.
3. The third cut to the branch collar.

New tissue forming over a wound.

The branch collar is the point at which the tree can best set up its protection against infection. It also provides strength for the branch with its overlapping trunk and branch tissue. Some collars are easy to see while others are more obscure. The collar is the point at the base of the branch where it changes thickness. It becomes more obvious when the branch decreases in vigor or begins to die.

Cutting at this point, known as target pruning, will mean that the cut is the minimum size. It will also prevent cutting through the natural defence zone that the collar provides. Cutting inside the collar by "flush cutting" will result in a bigger wound and the likelihood of disease and rot getting into the trunk. See figure 6.

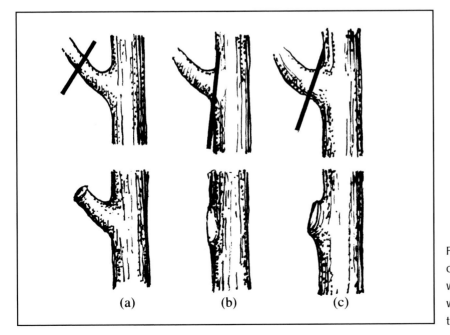

(a)   (b)   (c)

Fig. 6. Placement of the correct cut: (a) wrong − stub is left; (b) wrong − flush cut results in a big wound; (c) correct − target prune to collar.

Fig. 7. Crotch angles: (left) wide crotch angle – strong; (right) narrow crotch angle – weak.

Co-dominant stems with included bark. This union is weak.

If you prune to a collar, the tree will form new tissue over the wound naturally. Pruning paints and sealants are largely unnecessary if the correct pruning methods are used. In fact, these paints and sealants can provide an ideal environment for disease-causing organisms to enter the wound.

An understanding of how trees respond to wounding has been made clear through the work of Dr. Alex Shigo. Dr. Shigo spent many years as the chief research scientist with the U.S. Department of Agriculture and Forestry. He has written a number of books on tree biology and tree management, and continues to lecture and consult in many countries.

Dr. Shigo explains that trees have the ability to seal off damaged tissue so that the decay organisms do not invade sound wood. This process of sealing off an area of damaged tissue is called compartmentalizaton.

Form pruning

When obtaining seedling trees for planting, it is very important to select a specimen with good form. Trying to remedy a poorly formed tree at a later stage is far more difficult than when a young plant. Try to select trees with horizontal branching and avoid those with steep-angled branches. Branches with wide crotch angles are stronger than those with narrow angles. A crotch with a narrow angle is more likely to break off under a heavy load of fruit or in storms. If your plant has a narrow crotch angle, it is better to remove one of the branches at an early stage, as later on it will disfigure the tree. See figure 7.

On some trees you will see stems or trunks of about the same size originating from the same position from the main stem. These are called co-dominant stems. When the stem bark ridge turns upward the union is strong, but when it turns inward the union is weak. If the bark is turning inward, it is called included bark. Included bark is often associated with upright stems, especially in some trees such as *Liquidambar*. In this case the two stems are touching each other, but there is little actually holding them together. It is better to remove one of these stems if the union is weak, preferably when young. You will end up with a tree with a single dominant stem rather than one with co-dominant stems. See the photograph opposite showing co-dominant stems and included bark.

Timing

Except for some deciduous trees, most trees can be pruned at any time of the year. With some, such as flowering cherries and silver birches, pruning in early spring can result in heavy bleeding of sap from wounds. This bleeding can cause a loss of vigor and the moist wound may provide an entry point for disease organisms.

Stone-fruit, such as cherries, plums or nectarines, are prone to the fungal disease silverleaf if pruned in winter; the wet, cold conditions favor the spread of the fungal spores. It is better to prune in summer, as apart from reducing the risk of bleeding or infection, there are other advantages:

1. Wounds seal more quickly.
2. It is easier to identify deadwood and see the effect of pruning on the shape of the tree.

Timing can affect the vigor of the tree. For example, pruning a deciduous tree in late summer can reduce its vigor. This is because in late summer the tree hasn't had the chance to transport the food reserves from the leaves and to store them. It will have less food reserves in spring and less vigor in the short term.

Trees and the law

Being a good neighbor and a good citizen suggests some common sense ideas found in most legal systems relating to trees. However, it is impossible to deal with the complexities of local law across many jurisdictions. The advice given here is not formal legal advice, and readers should obviously take advice from a qualified lawyer on any matters locally.

Good neighbors
If you own land, you might think that you can do anything you want with your trees, and prevent anyone coming on to your land without your permission. But it is not always strictly true. Most countries recognize legal

Ulmus glabra

principles that say you have to use your land responsibly and without causing harm to your neighbors. For example, if your tree's branches overhang the neighbor's property, in principle you should prune the branches on your side to prevent overhang. Actually, the neighbor can often prune the tree from his or her side of the fence if you don't.

Wherever possible, it makes sense to talk to each other first, as the neighbor might not object anyway and even quite like the trees in that spot, branches and all. It all requires common sense and neighborliness. Similarly, your trees and your care of them should not harm a neighbor by things like pollen or spray drifting across the boundary, or branches or trunks falling on to a neighbor's house in high winds. In some circumstances you might be personally liable for the damage if you have not taken reasonable care to prevent the events.

Some situations give rise to considerable neighborhood tension and are actually quite complicated in law. A common example is a tree blocking the view or sunshine for a neighbor, even though the tree is entirely on one property and nothing is crossing the actual boundary. A general principle is that views and sunshine are not in fact protected against blocking by neighbors' trees, but check with the local authorities as there may be exceptions, depending on the locality. Remember also the laws protecting property against entry and self-help without the permission of the owner or lawful occupant — often known as the laws of trespass.

Generally (but alas not always!) principles of common sense neighborliness coincide with the law here, although it helps enormously if you can rely on others having common sense too, instead of reaching for the lawyers. Neighborhood disputes can turn into power games, wasting enormous emotional energy and money, sometimes even involving the police. Of course, the trees may be symptomatic of other problems in neighborly relations. I know a case in which two neighbors spent more than $80,000 over a tree dispute and the tree was valued at $200! A friendly chat with a neighbor may be worth a great deal in building relationships so that if a tree does become a major issue there is something in the neighborhood bank to draw on in getting cooperation.

Get professional advice from an arborist regarding the value of a tree on your property as well as how to be a good tree-neighbor in terms of pruning, care and so on. If there is a dispute over a tree, using an outside arborist might help to get good results for both sides, but nothing substitutes for good neighborliness.

Good citizens

Good citizens care for the future as well as the present, for their environment as well as for their neighbors. Trees have their place in all of that. In many areas, conservation and local planning laws have radically curbed any notion that current land-owners can cut everything down and burn it on their properties. Similar laws prevent the restriction of waterways, pollution of the soil or air, and so on. In a crowded world where urbanization appears to have no limit, there are no easy answers. But there is a growing international common sense that we should re-learn to live with, rather than destroy, our natural heritage. Much ink has been spilled (and many trees felled!) on sustainability. For me, its essence is about stewardship, meaning simply that we try to leave our grandchildren and those that follow, and indeed the many species with which we live, better, not worse, for our brief tenure of the land.

These notions affect trees at vital parts of the environmental debates. At a global level, we know that trees are the lungs of the planets and lots of energy is going into preserving forests and replanting deserts. But in cities and towns trees are also important to the environment. Green belts and city parks are often preserved for their beauty and a sense of nature among concrete, tar and brick (and, actually, as cleaners of the air, for shade, shelters and windbreaks). Individual huge old historic trees in gardens or streets are often regarded as so valuable for the locality that there are special designations put on them by local councils, preventing them from being pruned or cut down. Similarly, small but lovely stands of original forest might be preserved against cutting, even on private land. If you want a fine tree or stand on your land or in the neighborhood to be seen by future generations, check with your local council. It is better to get something preserved well in advance of a situation where they might have to be cut down for development. In the end, however, councils are only the creations of their voters and they rely on good citizenship, not least to protect trees.

In turn, both good neighborliness and good citizenship require common sense, in relation to trees as well as everything else.

An arborist at work.

Arborists

Larger tree work should be carried out by trained arborists. Arborists can train at training institutions and become members of their national arboriculture association. Using a contractor who is a member of this association gives clients some protection if things go wrong, as the association can ask the contractor to put it right.

> Ψ   Use an arborist if pruning involves climbing the tree.

3
Pruning techniques for other plants

Pruning techniques for shrubs

A shrub is a multibranched plant up to about 6 ft. (1.8 m) such as a rhododendron. (Some of the larger rhododendrons are trees.)

Ideally a shrub has a low, spreading crown. Pruning should aim to maintain a healthy crown and avoid the shrub becoming leggy and only flowering at the tips, leaving the base bare.

Evergreen shrubs

As with trees, you can remove the 3 Ds of dead, damaged and diseased wood. Most flowering evergreen shrubs should have their spent flowers removed. A good example is rhododendrons: remove the faded flowers before they turn to seed. This deadheading conserves the plant's energy and encourages further flowering. In the case of shrubs such as lavenders you can cut them back after the main flush of flowers. By removing about one-third of the growth you encourage bushiness and repeat flowering. Removing the end shoots like this is called heading back. Where possible, prune back to a node using pruning shears. See figure 9. While you can prune back shrubs like lavenders with hedge clippers (hedge shears), it is neater to prune using pruning shears.

Other than deadwooding and deadheading, ensure the shrub has a balanced growth habit and that it doesn't get too woody at the base. With shrubs like camellias you can remove taller growth or cut them back to lower branches to encourage growth nearer the ground. This will also encourage better flowering.

Deciduous shrubs

The golden rule is to prune after flowering. Pruning before flowering will remove potential flowers and fruit. Once the flowers are spent you can prune to encourage the right growth. Shrubs can either flower on the previous season's growth or on current season's growth.

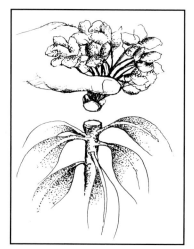

Fig. 8. Deadheading a rhododendron. Remove the flowers using thumb and finger.

Fig. 9. Heading back.

22

Flowering on the previous season's growth

These shrubs initiate their flowers in summer, and the flowers bloom the following spring. Shrubs in this category include *Forsythia* species and *Syringa* species (lilac). Prune them soon after flowering. Cut the old flowers and shoots back after flowering in spring so that the plant starts to branch, producing new flowering wood for the following year.

If you were to cut back these plants in winter, it would remove the majority of flower buds and result in a poor display of flowers the following summer.

Flowering on the current season's growth

These shrubs flower on current season's growth, which will produce flower buds. To encourage new growth, prune back in late winter or early spring, before bud break. Shrubs in this category include *Hibiscus* species and *Spiraea japonica* (Japanese spirea).

Hedges

The ideal hedge has dense, even growth from the top to bottom. Regular trimming on the sides will encourage this. Trimming hedges means cutting back the tip growth, usually with hedge clippers. You don't have to cut to nodes as you normally do with, say, roses. Trimmed hedges should be slightly wider at the base and slope in at the top. This allows light into the base of the plant, encouraging growth, as described below. Cutting back too hard or removing too much bottom growth can result in dieback.

To produce a hedge of the required height without allowing it to grow too high too quickly, you initially need to trim the sides to maintain dense growth. The tip growth can be lightly pruned to keep the growth dense, but allow the hedge to grow to the required height. Once the height is achieved the hedge can be cut across the top regularly. Hedges can be trimmed any time, but ideally after flowering if they flower or during the growing season if they don't. Different hedges will require different amounts of trimming,

Fig. 10. Correct ways of training a hedge. By having the hedge wider at the bottom, more light can get to the base of the plant and this reduces the chance of dieback.

23

Shrubs are not the only good subjects for a hedge. Above is a beech hedge (*Fagus sylvatica*) in winter.

depending on their rate of growth. Pre-winter and winter pruning are not a good idea in frost-prone areas as the resultant regrowth may be burned off.

Hedges require closer planting than normal to get the required density. For example, *Camellia sasanqua* can be planted 3 ft. (1 m) apart.

Conifers as hedges

If you cut conifers back too hard they will not regenerate as they rarely produce new shoots from old dormant wood. Only prune back to new growth. Dieback is often seen in conifer hedges that have been pruned too hard back into bare wood.

Taller conifers such as *Araucaria heterophylla* (syn. *A. excelsa*, Norfolk Island pine) cannot have their height reduced without ruining their symmetrical shape. For this reason make sure you plant such trees in places where they have maximum space to grow — not under power lines or near buildings!

The upright cypress *Cupressus sempervirens* 'Stricta' tends to open out with age. Often people will tie the fallout branches in using wire, but this looks ugly. You can avoid this by early training. Clip regularly and tuck in or cut out the fallout branches as they develop.

Topiary

Topiary is the technique of training plants into various shapes by clipping them. Plants suitable for topiary need to be relatively slow-growing, respond well to pruning and have a dense growth habit. They can be trained to form shapes such as cones or finely clipped hedges. Examples of suitable plants are *Buxus sempervirens* (box, boxwood), *Lonicera nitida* (Chinese honeysuckle), *Taxus baccata* (yew) and *Laurus nobilis* (bay). Deciduous specimens, although less popular than evergreen ones, include plants like *Crataegus monogyna* (hawthorn).

For deciduous plants such as hawthorn, cut them back hard for the first two years, and when the desired height is reached, prune each summer to maintain that height and shape.

Evergreen plants are not pruned in the first year other than removing untidy growth back to a collar or node. For the first three to four years prune to allow a 6–8 in. (15–20 cm) increase in height each year. Trim three to four times a year. Use secateurs for larger-leaved plants and hedge clippers for smaller leaved plants. Once mature, plants can be pruned once a year in late summer to keep their shape, or when they begin to look untidy.

The slow-growing *Buxus sempervirens* is an ideal subject for topiary.

Pruning techniques for climbers

The general principle of pruning after flowering applies to climbers.

Evergreen climbers need little pruning other than training them on to a suitable support structure and keeping them in bounds. Trim them back after flowering.

Climbers that flower on previous season's wood should be pruned after flowering by removing flowers and thinning out crowded shoots. Most of the climbers in this category, such as *Clematis montana*, flower in spring to early summer.

Climbers that flower on current season's wood such as *Bougainvillea* should be pruned in early spring. Remove all dead and damaged wood and prune back growth to a healthy bud.

Fig. 11. Training fruit trees. left to right: vase shape; centre leader; multi leader; espalier.

Pruning techniques for fruit trees

Pruning fruit plants involves trying to maximize fruit production as well as establish a healthy plant on a strong framework. Apart from removing the 3 Ds, you need to:

1. Get more light into the plant to encourage fruiting.
2. Remove old fruiting wood.
3. Control the plant's size.

You can train fruit trees in different ways:

Open center or vase method
Keep the center of the tree open, much as you would for bush roses.

Center-leader method
One central trunk is trained, with branches in tiers up the trunk.

Multi-leader method
Four or five leaders form the basic framework, with branches on the outside of the leaders.

25

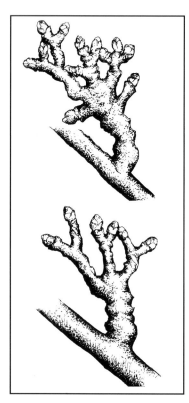

Fig. 12. Thinning apple spurs improves fruiting: (top) unpruned; (bottom) pruned.

Espalier method

The method you can use to train branches along a fence or along wires. Branches are selected and trained horizontally along wires. You can use different tiers to maximize the space. As the main fruiting branches are horizontal, you can encourage fruiting using this method.

Types of growth

You prune to encourage the type of growth on which flowering and fruiting takes place. The different types of growth are:

Fruiting on current season's growth

Plants such as *Actinidia deliciosa* (syn. *A. chinensis*, kiwifruit, Chinese gooseberry), *Feijoa sellowiana* (pineapple guava, feijoa) and grapes produce fruit on current season's growth. Cutting back of fruited wood is needed to encourage fruiting. Do not prune kiwifruit and grapes in late winter or early spring as excessive bleeding of sap can occur.

Fruiting on one-year-old wood

Many stone-fruit and berry fruit, such as peaches and raspberries, bear fruit on wood produced the previous season. Pruning involves removal of fruited wood. This will be replaced with new wood that will fruit the next year.

Fruiting on wood from the second year onwards

Apples, pears and apricots fruit on spurs for many years. Spurs are short laterals that end in flower buds (see figure 12). Pruning involves removing old tired spurs and removal of the 3 Ds. Little other pruning is required.

Cutting back delphiniums, such as *Delphinium* 'Blauer Zwerg', will encourage more flowers.

Pruning techniques for herbaceous perennials and bulbs

Although these plants are usually soft-stemmed, you often need to prune them with pruning shears or hedge clippers. There are a number of practices that will help your herbaceous perennials to grow and flower well.

Deadheading

Removing flowers as they fade will promote further flowering. This deadheading can be done progressively or by removing all the faded flowers at once and cutting the whole plant back. A good example of plants responding to this type of pruning would be daisies.

Deadheading also improves the appearance and vigor of the plant, so remove spent flowers regularly unless you are leaving them for seed collection.

When cutting flowers for garden displays, as with, for example, delphiniums, cut back to encourage further flowers.

Heading back

Many herbaceous perennials need heading back to keep them bushy, so check them regularly. Heading back after flowering with pruning shears or hedge clippers will keep plants like daisies compact and growing strongly from the base.

Allowing bulbs to die back

Resist the temptation to cut bulbs back. Those such as daffodils and lilies should be left until the old leaves and stalks have died back. If you remove them too soon, the food manufactured and stored in the leaves does not get a chance to return to the bulb for overwintering.

Lilium regale, and other bulbs, should be left to die back naturally once flowering has finished so the food stored in the leaves can return to the bulb.

Pruning plants in containers

As gardens become smaller, growing plants in containers becomes more popular. When using containers, good plant selection is essential. For example, you can grow a range of fruit trees, such as apples and nectarines, on dwarf rootstocks which keep the plants growth in check. Citrus plants do well in pots, as do grapes and figs. Patio roses are also suitable for containers.

Vigorous climbing plants, such as *Bougainvillea*, can be kept in check by using a container.

Whatever plant you choose, make sure you use a container of suitable size, keep the plant adequately supplied with water and provide it with a slow-release fertiliser.

Prune your plants as you would normally do, including the removal of deadwood. Pruning in containers often involves simply keeping the plant to the size and shape required. Container plants are also ideal for trying your hand at topiary. See the section on Pruning techniques for shrubs.

For climbing plants such as grapes, train and prune them as you would normally.

Standard plants will need regular clipping each year with secateurs to maintain the desired shape. Prune back any straggly growth to a node. Prune flowering standards once they have completed flowering.

Container-grown dwarf apple trees, 'Telemon' variety, ready for sale.

4

Plant care

No introduction on pruning would be complete without considering the care of plants. All too often arborists are called in to fix a problem that was due to incorrect care of the plant at an earlier stage.

Planting

Planting or transplanting trees and shrubs is the first step. Always check that the plant is suited to the conditions in which it is being planted. Consider its eventual size, given the other structures around it, such as buildings and power lines.

If the soil is poor, you can improve it by adding organic matter, except for plants like proteas, which prefer low-fertility soils. If drainage is poor, you may need to lay drains. It is better to prepare a whole site for planting rather than dig holes for each plant. Mulching to a depth of 3–4 in. (7.5–10 cm) will hold in the moisture and keep the weeds down. Do not put heaped grass clippings around the roots or around the base of the stem as this can lead to collar rot of the stem.

When planting or transplanting, make sure that you don't bury the base of the plant too deeply. Keep to the original level of the pot or the ground level in the case of a transplanted tree or shrub. If you mound up soil around the base of a tree you can kill it as the lack of air and excess moisture at the base can cause rot and failure. This is all too often a problem on building sites where excavation or filling is taking place around established trees.

Watering at the time of planting is very important. Regardless of the weather conditions at the time of planting, soak the plants with water to blend the fine soil particles around the disturbed root structure. Once this is done normal watering can take place as required. You can add a water retention material as well as a long-term fertilizer at the time of planting.

When staking, don't overstake. The purpose of staking is to hold the plant and reduce movement of the roots until the plant is established. If you stake too high or completely immobilize the tree you can weaken it by not allowing the tree to develop a self-supporting root structure. A good rule of thumb is to stake no higher than two-thirds up the trunk of the tree or shrub.

A newly planted tree, staked and mulched.

Once the tree is established firmly in the ground the stake can be removed. Care is needed when using wires to hold trees. Use a material like rubber to hold the tree to avoid it damaging the plant. If in doubt use a proprietary tree tie product.

Caring for and pruning plants in freezing conditions

When pruning in climates with severe frosts or heavy snow, you need to make allowances.

It is better to prune branches earlier, for example in fall rather than in winter. This is because heavy frosts cause freezing and thawing, which damages cells, and causes fissures or cracks in the bark tissue. Pruning in fall or earlier allows the wounds to harden up and seal over.

When pruning roses, the colder the winter, the later you should prune, to avoid new growth being damaged by late frosts.

In areas with heavy snow, trees such as *Cedrus libani* (cedar of Lebanon), which has long lateral branches, can have their length reduced. This is because the weight of the snow on the extra length of branch can cause the branch to break.

Deciduous trees such as *Erythrina* (coral tree) and herbaceous perennials, which die back each year, can have their roots covered with straw or similar material to reduce the likelihood of the roots freezing.

Root pruning

Remember that pruning includes roots, both when transplanting or excavating around plants.

When pruning roots use pruning shears or pruning saws to get a clean cut. Damaged roots can be entry points for disease. If you have transplanted a tree or shrub and had to remove roots, you can cut the shoot growth back to compensate for the reduced root growth. Pruning to reduce the amount of shoot growth when planting in exposed sites also has the benefit of

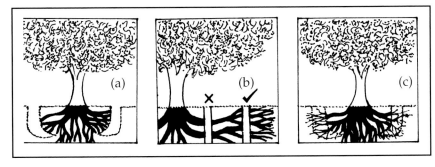

(a)　(b)　(c)

Fig. 13. Root pruning for transplanting. The correct sequence of events when root pruning a tree before transplanting: (a) dig trench around the tree; (b) cut roots neatly; (c) when new fibrous roots start to form, transplant.

29

reducing wind resistance. Don't cut back too much growth as the plant uses the leaves to manufacture food and re-establish itself.

A number of plants do not respond well to root pruning; some can bleed from the cuts. Examples include birches, cherries and maples. Some plants have roots that are sensitive to bruising, such as magnolias, making them difficult to transplant.

When transplanting plants that have been growing in the garden for a number of years, root prune before you shift the plant. Ideally make the shift when the plant is dormant. An early fall root prune allows for the best growth of new fibrous roots to nourish the plant after transplanting.

Transplanting method

The method for transplanting is:

1. Dig a trench around the plant. The size of the trench depends on the size of the plant and root development. Also, you need to be able to shift the rootball so consider its weight. Carefully dig around with a spade, cutting roots cleanly with pruning shears or a pruning saw as shown in figure 13.
2. Dig down until there are few roots and dig under this rootball.
3. Refill the trench with good-quality soil or sawdust. New fibrous roots will form during the growing season. Early to mid-fall is the best time for new root growth.
4. Prune back some of the foliage to compensate for a loss of roots. One school of thought is to leave pruning until it can be ascertained which part of the crown is affected by the root loss.
5. At transplanting, carefully undercut the rootball and lift. Holding the rootball in sacking will help to keep the soil in and keep it moist.
6. Keeping the soil moist and the leaves misted will reduce any transplanting shock. You can buy anti-transpiration agents that reduce water loss from the leaves.

Plant health

A plant's health is much like our own. If we are under stress we are more likely to become sick. Similarly, if plants are under stress due to lack of water or air, for example, then they are more likely to be affected by pests or diseases or show a check in growth. Often the effect of damage or poor plant management practices can take years to manifest.

Providing the right environmental conditions for your plants is essential for optimum growth. Practices such as mulching, weeding, adding fertilizers, watering and pruning, if correctly done, will favor the growth of your plants. Good hygiene, by removing diseased or infested material and burning or sending it to a waste disposal site, helps to remove a future

A beautiful example of a mulberry tree (*Morus nigra*). Good garden maintenance through pruning for the 3 Ds will ensure this tree remains an asset for many years.

source of infection or infestation. If you are pruning a diseased plant, remove the infected parts.

Pruning at certain times will mean it is less likely that diseases will spread. For example, pruning stone-fruit in summer to early fall when it is warm and dry will mean that the spores of the fungal disease silverleaf won't be present.

Environmental factors such as light, temperature, moisture and wind also affect plant growth. Each plant has an ideal set of conditions. If one of these factors is not ideal it can result in poor growth. For example, planting a sun-loving plant in the shade can make it soft and drawn, while planting a shade-loving plant in the sun can cause scorching or yellowing. Strong salt-laden wind or frost can cause similar physical damage to plants, even though the environmental conditions are quite different. While you can undertake remedial pruning on a plant that has become drawn due to low light conditions, or has been damaged by wind, it is better to grow it in ideal conditions in the first place.

If plants are prone to certain pests or diseases, this will be mentioned under the specific plant in Part Two.

5
Tools

I know from experience that it is better to pay the extra money and buy quality tools. Poor-quality tools are frustrating to use as they won't do the job as efficiently. The important thing to remember is to use the tool for its intended purpose. If you have to strain a tool to do the job you can damage the tool and/or the plant. For example, when using a pair of pruning shears, you shouldn't have to strain or twist them to cut through material. Rather than do this, it would be more appropriate to use loppers or a pruning saw.

Pruning shears (secateurs)

Pruning shears or secateurs are best used for material up to ⅜ in. (1 cm) in diameter. They are ideal for pruning roses and shrubs.

There are two types of pruning shears: parrot-beak and anvil. The parrot-beak pruning shears are made from two curved blades, one of which is sharp and thin, the other thicker. The two blades pass one another. It is a good idea to use the sharp side to cut into the branch, leaving the back blade to hold the back of the branch.

There are now many models of parrot-beak pruning shears, such as left-hand ones or a swivel handle model that gives more comfort and flexibility in use.

The anvil or rollcut pruning shears have a straight blade that cuts against a flat surface or anvil. This type has a tendency to crush stems compared with the parrot-beak type.

Loppers

Loppers are effectively long-handled pruning shears with each handle held in a separate hand. This gives them more leverage and cutting power than pruning shears.

They come with handles of different sizes, but are typically 18 in. (45 cm) long. Like pruning shears they come in the parrot-beak or anvil type cutting action. Some larger models have a double action, which gives a lot more leverage and power.

Loppers are ideal for stems up to 1⅜ in. (3.5 cm), although the double-action lopper can cut thicker stems.

The pole pruner has blades at the end of a long pole. The blades are closed by a wire or cord operated from the foot of the handle. This tool is ideal for pruning branches that are out of reach of the normal pruning shears or loppers.

Saws

Pruning saws are designed specifically for pruning and can cut through green, wet wood. Don't use a carpenter's saw unless you want to make the job difficult. They are designed for cutting dry wood. Most pruning saws have curved blades and cut on the backward stroke, or have a double-action cut, unlike the carpenter's saw which works on a push stroke only. The curved blades make it easier to get into tight corners of trees. Pruning saws are suitable for cutting branches that can't be cut using loppers.

There are many different saws, but the bow saw (right) and curved saws are commonly used for arboricultural work. The bow saw is a sturdy saw that works on a push-and-pull stroke. While ideal for cutting bigger branches, it is not so suitable for cutting in confined spaces.

Folding curved saws are ideal for pruning smaller plants and have the advantage of fitting in your pocket. Rigid-handle curved saws are suitable for heavier work. Some models have cases to fit the saw in, which protects the saw but also allows the saw to be attached to your belt. This has the added advantage of lessening the chances of losing your saw — a common problem with saws and pruning shears!

Hedge clippers

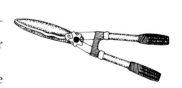

Hedge clippers or shears are used for clipping hedges, for topiary, and for heading back some shrubs such as lavenders.

Check that the blades are stainless steel, and that the blades can be tightened easily, usually with a nut and bolt. The handles can be metal or wooden, and should have a shock absorber between the handles just beneath the blade's pivot point to make cutting easier on your hands.

Hedge trimmers

For larger hedges, or for commercial work, gas (petrol) or electricity-driven trimmers can be used. The electric models can either be cordless, battery operated, or incorporate a cord from the mains. The battery model is suitable for smaller hedges such as *Buxus*, box or boxwood, while the cord model can handle bigger hedges. As with all electrical equipment, use a circuit breaker and take care not to cut or damage the cord.

Gas-driven models are more powerful than electrical models, but are heavier and require skill to operate. Ear protection is needed, so check your local standard requirements for the correct grade of earmuff to be used. Eye protection such as goggles is also a good idea.

Don't treat these machines lightly, as serious injuries can result.

Chainsaws (power saws)

No section on tools would be complete without mention of chainsaws or power saws. A lot could be said about chainsaws, but before starting these powerful tools, you should have been instructed in the safe use of them by a qualified instructor or agent for the saw manufacturer.

It hardly needs mentioning that a cut from a chainsaw will do a lot more damage to your body than a pruning saw. If using chainsaws use all the necessary protective gear, and do not climb trees with chainsaws without using safety harnesses and ropes. In fact, leave the use of chainsaws off the ground to professionals.

Using sharp pruning saws to cut branches can be very effective, and can also give you more time to reflect on the effect of each cut. It is far too easy to run amok when presented with the convenience and awesome power of a chainsaw for use as a pruning tool.

Opposite: *Fuchsia paniculata*

PART TWO

TECHNIQUES FOR PRUNING SOME POPULAR GARDEN PLANTS

The symbol Ψ indicates that an arborist should be used to prune the plant.

Abelia x *grandiflora*

Abelia x *grandiflora*

Abelia, glossy abelia

FAMILY: CAPRIFOLIACEAE

hardiness rating: 6–9

This hybrid of abelia and favorite cultivars such as *Abelia* 'Francis Mason' are popular as hedges. They are hardy to cold and grow in sun or semi-shade. The hybrid grows to 7 ft. (2.1 m), the cultivars to about 4 ft. (1.2 m).

The flowers are white with a pink tinge, appearing if the plant is left untrimmed.

Pruning

If using as a hedge, plant 12–18 in. (30–45 cm) apart and train to the required height, about 3–7 ft. (1–2.1 m). The soft growth makes trimming with hedge clippers very easy. Trim back two or three times a year.

If using abelia as a shrub, cut it back hard each year after flowering. Cut back by one-half to a node. Hard pruning will encourage new growth and flowering. If left unpruned, abelias can become leggy and woody.

Propagation

From softwood cuttings in the spring.

Abies concolor subsp. *lowiana*

Abies

Fir

FAMILY: PINACEAE

hardiness rating: 5–9

These evergreen conifers are from the Northern Hemisphere. The name comes from the Latin *abies*, a fir tree. They grow to 100–200 ft. (30–60 m), and are ideal as specimens or they can be kept small as container plants. They differ from spruces in that the leaves come away cleanly from the branch, and the cones are upright.

Firs are cold hardy, and prefer soils with adequate moisture. *Abies grandis* (giant fir, lowland fir) and *A. nordmanniana* (Nordmann fir) are tolerant of lime, while *A. concolor* (white fir), *A. pinsapo* (Spanish fir) and *A. procera* (noble fir) prefer lime-free soils.

Pruning Ψ

These trees need little pruning other than the removal of deadwood.

If the central leader gets damaged, you can prune back to another suitable lateral branch. Using a pruning saw, cut above the new branch at an angle.

Propagation

From seed, stratifying them for 8–12 weeks.

Acacia (syn. *Racosperma*)

Acacia, mimosa, wattle

FAMILY: FABACEAE

hardiness rating: 8–11

Popular garden varieties of these mostly evergreen trees come mainly from Australia. The name is derived from the Greek *akis*, meaning a sharp point or thorn, referring to the thorny species, such as *Acacia paradoxa* (syn. *A. armata*, kangaroo thorn). *A. baileyana* (Cootamundra wattle) doesn't have thorns and provides intense yellow flowers in winter. It grows to 30 ft. (9 m). *A. cardiophylla* is smaller at only 9–12 ft. (3–4 m).

Wattles are tolerant of dry soils and full sunlight. They grow quickly and require little fertilizer. They are prone to unsightly galls, which are caused by rust fungi.

Acacia baileyana

Pruning Ψ
Pruning after flowering will help to encourage new growth and will also contribute to better displays. Only prune back to a node behind the flowers as wattles prefer light pruning. Once the tree is the desired shape, prune regrowth to maintain this. If there is insufficient light at the base of the tree, dieback can occur. If this happens, remove growth back to the collar. Crown-cleaning or crown-raising will help to get more light back into the tree.

Wattles are prone to wind damage, so if this happens, prune back to a collar. Because they are shallow-rooted, they are prone to blowing over, so in a windy environment staking at planting may be necessary for a short time to help them get established.

Propagation
From seed, but soak seeds in hot water to improve germination.

Acer
Maple
FAMILY: ACERACEAE
hardiness rating: 4–9

This genus of Northern Hemisphere deciduous plants has colorful spring growth and often brilliant fall shades. The name comes from the Latin *acer*, sharp, referring to the hard wood that was used in Roman spear shafts. The many cultivars of *Acer palmatum* (Japanese maple) and *A. palmatum* 'Dissectum' provide a large range of color and form. *A. campestre* (hedge maple) grows to 50 ft. (15 m), *A. griseum* (paperbark maple) reaches 6–8 ft. (1.8–2.4 m), while *A. negundo* (ash-leaved maple, box elder, Manitoba maple), is a fast-growing tree to 50 ft. (15 m). *A. platanoides* (Norway maple) and *A. saccharinum* (silver maple, soft maple) are both very vigorous growers, each reaching 80 ft. (25 m).

Acer palmatum

Maples need well-drained, lime-free soil with adequate moisture over summer. They do not tolerate strong wind as it burns the foliage. Give them a sheltered site and placed them where their attractive features can be appreciated. The weeping maples can be grown in a container.

Pruning Ψ
Maples do not need regular pruning. Once their shape is established, keep them healthy and free of the 3 Ds. They can be crown-raised or reduced depending on the situation (see Introduction).

Be careful with your timing as pruning maples in late winter and spring can result in bleeding of the sap.

If the variegated types revert to green, remove this growth. Sometimes the bark of maples can split. If it does, then carefully clean around the wound with a sharp knife to remove loose or flaky tissue, taking care not to damage sound tissue underneath. Leave the wound to seal naturally.

A. saccharinum is prone to included bark (inwardly formed bark at the junction of branches or co-dominant stems; this union is inherently weak).

Propagation

A. palmatum can be grown from seed that has been chilled in the refrigerator for two months. The many cultivars are grafted.

Actinidia deliciosa

Actinidia deliciosa (syn. *A. chinensis*)
Chinese gooseberry, kiwifruit, kiwi vine

FAMILY: Actinidiaceae

hardiness rating: 7–9

This popular deciduous vine is well known commercially. The name comes from the Greek *aktis*, a ray, referring to the flower. *A. deliciosa* is also known as *A. chinensis*. *Chinensis* refers to its country of origin, hence the common name Chinese gooseberry. The vine can be trained up a trellis or pergola. Separate male and female vines are needed to produce fruit; however, plants with both male and female on the same plant can be purchased.

Kiwifruit need full sun, good drainage and adequate moisture over the summer period. They are very vigorous growers and may need a general fertilizer each year.

Pruning

Because kiwifruit are so vigorous, they need training and pruning to prevent them becoming a tangled mass.

Firstly, establish a framework, depending on your chosen structure. For example, you could use a pergola. Once the vine is trained up to the required height, select strong canes and tie them down horizontally. These fruiting canes need thinning in summer to allow maximum light for fruit ripening, so shorten the canes back to the nearest node. In winter, prune back old shoots to the main vine to encourage new growth. Remember that, like grapes, kiwifruit should not be pruned in late winter or early spring as they can bleed heavily.

Kiwifruit are very hardy and vigorous and older vines can be cut back severely to rejuvenate them if they have got out of control. Train one male plant with female plants, or use a plant with both male and female to ensure pollination.

Propagation

From semi-ripe stem cuttings taken in summer or hardwood cuttings in winter. The semi-ripe cuttings need adequate misting but hardwood cuttings can be left outdoors in a free-draining mix.

Aesculus
Buckeye, horse chestnut

FAMILY: HIPPOCASTANACEAE

hardiness rating: 3–8

These deciduous trees are from Southeast Europe, North America and Northeast Asia. The name *aesculus* comes from the Latin word for winter oak. They are ideal as specimen trees. *Aesculus hippocastanum* (common horse chestnut) grows to a large, spreading tree. *A.* x *carnea* (red horse chestnut) is a beautiful tree with deep pink flowers that is smaller than *A. hippocastanum*. *A. flava* (syn. *A. octandra*, yellow buckeye) is a large tree from North America, while *A. pavia* (syn. *A. splendens*, red buckeye) is a smaller tree from Southern United States.

They prefer rich, moist soils, shelter from strong winds, and can grow in sun or semi-shade.

Aesculus hippocastanum

Pruning Ψ

These trees need little pruning, other than removal of the 3 Ds. Ideally they should be trained with a central leader, and any inferior leaders pruned back to the branch collar. They can also be crown-raised to get more room around the base of the tree, by cutting back lower branches to the collar using a pruning saw. Remember to undercut the branch before making the final cut. They are noted for having fragile branches and heartwood that rots out quickly.

Propagation

From seed, which has been stratified for 12 weeks. Cultivars are grafted.

Agathis australis
Dammar pine, kauri, kauri pine

FAMILY: ARAUCARIACEAE

hardiness rating: 9–11

This evergreen conifer is from New Zealand. The name *agathis* refers to the shape of the cone (like a ball of thread), while *australis* means southern. This slow-growing, large tree is tolerates frosts and heavy clay soils. Very large trees (over a thousand years old) were milled for timber in New Zealand in the 19th and 20th centuries; however, its slow growth means it can be used as a specimen tree, or in mixed planting.

Pruning Ψ

Little pruning is needed. Younger trees shed their branches naturally, leaving a clean trunk as the tree matures.

Propagation
From seed.

Agathis australis

Agonis juniperina

Agonis
Willow myrtle

FAMILY: MYRTACEAE

hardiness rating: 10–11

This is a genus of evergreen trees and shrubs from Western Australia. The word *agon* means gathering or collection, referring to the number of seeds. Frost tender when young, surviving light frosts when mature, these plants are drought hardy and tolerate limey soils. They grow to 14–18 ft. (4–5.5 m), and can be used as a specimen or in mixed planting. *Agonis juniperina* (small-leaved willow myrtle) is used for cut flowers, being short-lived but having persistent flowers.

Pruning Ψ

A. flexuosa (peppermint tree, willow myrtle) can have its crown reduced or raised, depending on the desired effect. Lower branches should be cut to a collar using a pruning saw.

A. *juniperina* can be cut back about one-third each year after flowering to maintain a bushy habit. Cut back branches to a node with pruning shears or loppers. This multibranched tree has a habit of shedding branches and, if left unpruned, can become untidy.

Propagation

From seed, semi-ripe cuttings or from grafting for the variegated cultivars.

Ailanthus altissima

Ailanthus altissima
Tree of heaven

FAMILY: SIMAROUBACEAE

hardiness rating: 4–8

The genus includes deciduous trees from South and Eastern Asia and Australia, but *A. altissima* (tree of heaven) from China is the main one grown. The word *ailanto* means sky tree, while *altissima* means very tall, as the tree grows to 60 ft. (18 m).

It is very pollution hardy and resistant to most pests and diseases. It features large leaves, and the male plant has flowers with a disagreeable odour. Hence, female plants are recommended. It can sucker badly in light soils, so is best used in open spaces. In small gardens its suckering habit needs to be strictly controlled.

Pruning Ψ

If grown as a tree, little pruning other than removal of the 3 Ds is required. The tree can be cut back to ground level each spring in smaller gardens, after which it will quickly produce the attractive large leaves.

Propagation

From seed or root cuttings. The more desirable female plant can be propagated only vegetatively from root cuttings.

Akebia quinata
Chocolate vine, fiveleaf akebia

FAMILY: LARDIZABALACEAE
hardiness rating: 5–9

This climber, native to Japan, China and Korea, is evergreen in milder climates and deciduous elsewhere. It prefers a free-draining soil, and tolerates sun or shade. The purplish chocolate-colored flowers are vanilla scented.

Pruning

Cut back the long healthy shoots to a node from winter to early spring. Trim weak or dead growth to a collar or node. In milder climates, where growth is rapid, it can be cut almost to ground level each year in fall.

Training

It is better to train this climber up a structure such as a trellis fence. It can become difficult to manage if allowed to grow up a tree, and may even smother and destroy the host.

Akebia quinata

Propagation

From seed, or soft or semi-ripe stem cuttings in spring and summer.

Alnus
Alder

FAMILY: BETULACEAE
hardiness rating: 5–8

These mostly deciduous trees come from the Northern Hemisphere. The name *alnus* comes from the Latin for alder. Commonly grown species include *Alnus cordata* (Italian alder) from Italy and *A. glutinosa* (black alder, common alder) from Europe. *A. jorullensis* from Central America is the only semi-evergreen species. They tolerate wet soils with low fertility, as their roots fix their own nitrogen. They are ideal as shade or shelter trees in moist soils or near waterways.

Pruning Ψ

Little pruning is required if grown as a specimen, other than raising the crown, and removing the 3 Ds. If grown as shelter trees, the spreading branches can be cut back to suitable lateral branches to maintain a denser, more compact growth. Loppers or pruning saws can be used to do this.

Alnus glutinosa

Propagation

Mostly from seed that has been stratified for 12 weeks.

Amelanchier
Juneberry, shadbush, snowy mespilus, serviceberry

FAMILY: ROSACEAE
hardiness rating: 4–9

These deciduous small trees are mostly from the United States. They grow in sun or shade, are frost hardy, and prefer a lime-free, moisture-retentive

41

Amelanchier lamarckii

free-draining soil. They are notable for their rich fall foliage and showy white flowers in spring.

Amelanchier canadensis (shadblow, shadbush), *A. laevis* (Allegheny serviceberry) and *A. lamarckii* all reach about 20 ft. (6 m), but *A. canadensis* has a more suckering habit.

Pruning Ψ

As *A. canadensis* is a suckering shrub, it should have the oldest stems cut back to the collar in winter. *A. laevis* and *A. lamarckii* can be trained as trees by raising the crown, cutting back the lower branches to the collar with a pruning saw. (Use an arborist for *A. laevis* and *A. lamarckii* if climbing is involved.)

Propagation

From seed that has been stratified for 12 weeks, or from division of *A. canadensis* in late winter.

Araucaria heterophylla (syn. *A. excelsa*)
Norfolk Island pine

FAMILY: ARAUCARIACEAE

hardiness rating: 9–10

This large tree, native to Norfolk Island, is related to the kauri and monkey puzzle (Chilean pine) tree. The species name *heterophylla* means different leaves, referring to the different juvenile and adult foliage. It is suitable for coastal planting. Because of its tall, pyramidal shape it needs adequate space to grow upwards and outwards. It can grow to 200 ft. (60 m) high with a wide spread. Young plants may need staking or some other form of wind protection to help them become established. The Norfolk Island pine can also be used as a container plant indoors.

Pruning Ψ

Like their relatives, the monkey puzzle and the kauri, these trees need little pruning. The important point is to plant them in the right place to start with. There is nothing more heart-breaking than to see one of these stately trees planted under a power line or too close to a house. In cases like this it is better to remove the tree rather than compromise its characteristic shape with severe pruning.

While you cannot reduce the height of the Norfolk pine without destroying its shape, you can train another leader if the original one is damaged. You can also raise the crown by removing the lower whorls of branches. This is important if access is required underneath. You can also remove alternate whorls of branches to open up the tree, improving the view or light. Dead and damaged branches should be removed back to the collar. Like all pines, the cuts will produce a sticky resin that can leave its mark on you.

Araucaria heterophylla

Propagation
From seed placed upright in a tray of seed mix.

Arbutus
Manzanita, strawberry tree, madrone

FAMILY: ERICACEAE
hardiness rating: 7–9

Arbutus unedo

These evergreen trees from Europe, the Mediterranean and the Middle East include the popular *Arbutus unedo* (strawberry tree) and *A.* x *andrachnoides*, which is a hybrid. *A. menziesii* (madrona tree, madroño) is used in Europe and the United States. The name *arbutus* relates to tree, while *unedo* means "I eat", as the fruit is edible.

Strawberry trees prefer moisture-retentive soils, but unlike other members of the Ericaceae family, which prefer acidic soils, *A. unedo* and *A.* x *andrachnoides* tolerate alkaline soils. While they are tolerant of coastal breezes, they do need protection from cold winds. All are suitable as specimen trees, or they can be used in background planting.

They are prone to damage from thrips, which cause silvering of the leaves.

Pruning Ψ
Remove deadwood, or any growth damaged by frosts or storms, back to the collar with a pruning saw.

Propagation
From seed or semi-ripe cuttings.

Azalea (see *Rhododendron*)

Banksia
Banksia

FAMILY: PROTEACEAE
hardiness rating: 8–11

Banksia 'Giant Candles'

Banksias are evergreen shrubs and trees native to Australia. Their bright flowers are very attractive in winter and spring.

They are members of the protea family, which prefer very free-draining, slightly acidic soils low in phosphorus. Ideally, they grow on a hot, sunny bank in poor soil. If the soil becomes waterlogged, it can be fatal. Likewise, if phosphate or lime is applied, it can be damaging or fatal.

They are very difficult to transplant so finding the right site is important, as is minimizing root loss during the transfer.

Pruning Ψ
Larger species like *Banksia integrifolia* (coast banksia) can have their shape and size controlled, allowing for their natural form. Like many of the protea family, they should not be cut back further than new growth unless you are removing larger branches, which can be taken back to the branch collar. If you cut back into branches past the new growth, dieback may result.

43

Some species such as *B. baxteri* have a tuberous root or lignotuber. The lignotuber stores food and contains buds that will grow if the top part of the plant is damaged. Banksias with lignotubers can be pruned to ground level and will generally regrow.

Propagation

From seed that has been soaked in water for about three days.

Berberis thunbergii 'Rose Glow'

Berberis
Barberry

FAMILY: BERBERIDACEAE

hardiness rating: 3–9

These evergreen and deciduous shrubs are from Asia, Europe and the Americas. The word *berberys* is from the Arabic for fruit. They are ideally grown among other shrubs to display their foliage and berries.

Some useful species are:

- *Berberis dictyophylla*, a deciduous shrub growing to 7 ft. (2.1 m).
- *B.* x *stenophylla*, an evergreen shrub growing to 8 ft. (2.4 m).
- *B. thunbergii* (Japanese barberry), a deciduous shrub growing to 8 ft. (2.4 m), with many cultivars such as *B. thunbergii* 'Atropurpurea'.
- *B. verruculosa* (warty barberry), an evergreen shrub to 5 ft. (1.5 m).

They prefer full sun, and grow in poor, wet soils. In poor soils they will produce a more prolific crop of berries, while better soils will produce more foliage.

Pruning

The evergreen species can be trained as hedges, using hedge clippers to trim them. If growing the evergreen shrubs for flowers or fruit, wait until the fruits have faded, and then cut back the long shoots by one-half to a node, using pruning shears. You may wish to use gloves when handling the spiny leaves. Prune deciduous plants after flowering. With all plants, remove old stems back to the base, and shorten spindly growth back to maintain the shape of the plant.

Propagation

From seed or from stem cuttings.

Betula pendula

Betula
Birch

FAMILY: BETULACEAE

hardiness rating: 2–9

A genus of deciduous trees and shrubs from the cooler Northern Hemisphere notable for their attractive bark and graceful habit. The more common *Betula pendula* (European white birch, silver birch), which grows to 27– 70 ft. (8–21 m), has pendulous or weeping branches as the name suggests. *B. pendula* 'Youngii' (Young's weeping birch) has a more pronounced weeping habit.

Birches don't have roots that rob the soil of nutrients or fill drains, as do willows. Wherever possible, they should be planted in groups of at least three to provide a mass display. They can tolerate wind and cold, but need moisture over the drier periods, especially in the first few years. Strong winds during the growing season can cause pronounced wind shear in the crown.

Pruning Ψ

If planted in the correct location, little pruning should be needed other than removing the 3 Ds. If the leader is broken, replace it with the nearest strong-growing shoot. Prune with a sloping cut away from the node.

Birches can be crown-raised to provide better access or light underneath, especially if single specimens. As for any trees that are planted in groups, ensure that branches are not distorting the growth of other trees.

Pruning should ideally be carried out in summer as pruning in late winter or early spring can cause sap bleeding. Pruning in winter could result in the development and spread of silverleaf disease.

Propagation

From the small, abundant seed. Sow the trays outdoors as the cool conditions simulate its natural environment.

Boronia
Boronia

FAMILY: RUTACEAE

hardiness rating: 9–10

Boronias are members of the same family as lemons and breath-of-heaven, with scented leaves and spring flowers. Mostly native to Australia, they all grow to around 4 to 6 ft. (1.2–2 m).

Boronia denticulata has lilac-mauve flowers, whereas *B. heterophylla* has rose-red blooms. *B. megastigma* (brown boronia, scented boronia) has flowers that are brown-purple on the outside and yellow within.

Boronia denticulata
'Sunset Serenade'

They need moisture over dry periods, but will often fail due to water-logging over winter. Adequate drainage is essential, but using a layer of mulch over the summer period will help to keep the roots cool and moist. Boronias are, however, temperamental plants can curl up their toes and die very suddenly.

Pruning

The flowers are ideal for cutting, providing a suitable length of stem. Like other evergreen shrubs blooming on new growth, they benefit from cutting back after flowering. Cut back to about one-half, after flowers have faded, to encourage new growth and flowers, and to maintain a bushy habit.

Cutting back too hard or too late in the season can cause dieback, so it is best to trim immediately after flowering.

Propagation

From semi-ripe stem cuttings taken in late summer to fall.

Brachyscome multifida

Brachyscome (syn. *Brachycome*)
Rock daisy, Swan River daisy

FAMILY: Asteraceae

hardiness rating: 10–11

The evergreen, low-growing annuals and perennials of this genus are mostly from Australia. The name *brachyscome* comes from the Greek *brachys* for short and *kome* for hair, alluding to the flower. *Brachyscome multifida* (rock daisy) and its many cultivars are perennials commonly grown for their deep blue flowers. They grow in sun or semi-shade, and need a free-draining soil with adequate moisture in dry periods.

Pruning
When the flowers have faded, cut back about one-half, using hedge clippers. This will encourage new growth and maximum flowering.

Propagation
Annuals from seed and perennials from tip cuttings.

Buddleja davidii

Buddleja (syn. *Buddleia*)
Buddleia, buddleja

FAMILY: Loganiaceae

hardiness rating: 6–10

Deciduous and evergreen plants of this genus come from Asia, North America and Africa. While there are subtropical species, the ones from China and India are most commonly cultivated. They are very hardy, and grow rapidly in warm conditions with moist soils. Buddlieas are grown for their fragrant flowers, and as a food source for monarch butterflies.

Pruning
This is dependent on the flowering habits of the plant.
- Those that flower on last year's growth, such as the deciduous *Buddleja alternifolia*, should be cut back after flowering. Cut back to nodes where there is new growth, using pruning shears.
- Those that flower at the end of shoots produced in the current year, such as *B. davidii* (butterfly bush, summer lilac) and its cultivars should be pruned in winter, cutting back the plant with loppers or pruning saw to 12 in. (30 cm).
- Those that grow strong shoots in one year and flower the next on buds from this growth, such as the evergreen *B. globosa* (orange ball tree), should have weak growth pruned back to branch collars in early spring, using a pruning saw.

Propagation
From seed, or from stem cuttings if a cultivar of *B. davidii*.

Buxus sempervirens

Buxus
Box, boxwood

FAMILY: Buxaceae

hardiness rating: 5–9

These evergreen shrubs are from the Northern Hemisphere. *Buxus* is Latin for box. They are very hardy, provided they have adequate drainage. Box is traditionally used for hedging, especially *Buxus sempervirens* (common boxwood), and is ideal for topiary and parterres. Another popluar species is *B. microphylla* (Japanese box), which grows to 10 ft. (3 m) and has leaves that turn yellow-brown in cold weather.

Box is prone to a fungal disease that manifests as black spots on the leaves, often leading to dead branches or death of the plant. Ensure the plants are well-drained, have adequate light, and do not water overhead.

Pruning
If grown as a shrub, *Buxus* need little pruning other than removal of the 3 Ds. If growing *Buxus sempervirens* as a hedge, clip it once a year in summer. Old plants can be cut back to 4 in. (10 cm) in early spring and have fertilizer applied when in growth. *Buxus sempervirens* 'Suffriticosa' (edging boxwood) needs trimming two or three times a year during the growing season.

Propagation
From stem cuttings taken in late spring to early fall.

Calliandra
Powderpuff tree, fairy dusters

FAMILY: FABACEAE

hardiness rating: 10–12

These evergreen shrubs and small trees are from tropical and subtropical America, Africa and India. The name *calliandra* comes from the Greek words *kallos*, meaning beauty, and *andros*, meaning stamens. They are grown for their showy flowers and feathery leaves. Common species include *Calliandra tweediei* (red tassel flower, Mexican flame bush), *C. portoricensis* (snowflake acacia) from Puerto Rico and *C. californica* (Baja fairy duster) from California.

They should be grown in full sun with free-draining soils. The plant is tender and requires a minimum of 55°F (13°C). Grow under eaves in a sunny position to provide light, drier conditions and some frost protection.

Calliandra portoricensis

Pruning
To maintain a bushy shape and improved flowering, prune shrubs lightly after flowering. Trim back to a suitable lateral branch with pruning shears.

Propagation
From stem cuttings.

Callicarpa
Beautyberry

FAMILY: VERBENACEAE

The mostly deciduous shrubs in this genus are from North America, Asia, Indonesia and Australia. The name *callicarpa* comes from the Greek *kalli* for beautiful and *karpos* for fruit. They are grown for their colorful fruit. Species

Callicarpa dichotoma 'Purpurea'

include *Callicarpa dichotoma* (Chinese beautyberry, purple beautyberry), *C. americana* (beautyberry, French mulberry), and *C. japonica.*

They prefer full sun, a free-draining alkaline soil.

Pruning

Keep plants to a desired shape by pruning after flowering to a suitable node with pruning shears. Older plants that have become straggly can be cut back hard to suitable nodes by late winter, using a pruning saw.

Propagation

From stem cuttings or seed.

Callistemon citrinus

Callistemon

Bottlebrush

FAMILY: Myrtaceae

hardiness rating: 9–11

A genus of attractive flowering shrubs from Australia. The name *Callistemon*, beautiful stamen, refers to the flowers, which are composed of showy stamens. The common name, bottlebrush, refers to the resemblance of the flower to a bottlebrush.

Callistemon citrinus 'Splendens' (crimson bottlebrush) is grown for its bright scarlet flowers. *C. viminalis* (weeping bottlebrush) has scarlet-crinsom blooms and an attractive weeping habit. Their leathery, scented leaves give these plants tolerance to the dry, hot conditions typical of their native habitat. Their woody seed capsules act as a protective device as the seeds are only dispersed after a fire, a common occurrence in Australia.

Pruning

Some bottlebrushes, such as *C. citrinus*, can be trained as a hedge. They can be kept to a height of 3–5 ft. (1–1.5 m). Plant about 3 ft. (1 m) apart and trim the back and sides with hedge clippers.

When pruning the shrubs, try to keep a dense, bushy growth. If you leave the flowers, they will form woody capsules that look unsightly. Also, leaving the plants unpruned can result in a spindly plant with little or no bottom growth. Pruning involves cutting back just past the spent flowers to a healthy node. Don't cut back too far into old wood otherwise you may not get regrowth. Old, spindly plants can be cut to ground level, as there is a high probability of rejuvenating growth.

Propagation

From seed, but cultivars are propagated from semi-ripe stem cuttings taken in fall.

Calluna vulgaris 'Darkness'

Calluna vulgaris

Heather, ling

FAMILY: Ericaceae

hardiness rating: 5–7

This evergreen shrub is from North America and Europe. The name *calluna* comes from the Greek word *kalluna*, to sweep or clean, in reference to their use as brooms. There is only one species of *Calluna*, but there are many cultivars, ideally used in a mixed planting for their flower color.

Heathers are very hardy, preferring full sun and a lime-free soil. They will tolerate wet and cold or hot and dry conditions. They may survive in Zone 3 with winter protection or sufficient snow cover.

Pruning
Trim these plants back by one-half after flowering, cutting back to a suitable node with pruning shears. You can also use hedge clippers, to ensure you get an even shape.

Propagation
From seed or stem cuttings.

Camellia
Camellia

FAMILY: THEACEAE
hardiness rating: 7–8

Camellias are members of the tea family originating from Asia. There is a huge range of size, flower color and form. *Camellia japonica* (common camellia) and its many cultivars are the most popular. *C. sasanqua* can be used as a hedge. Camellias prefer partial shade, good drainage and an acidic soil. Ideally, they need an organic soil, such as peat. As they are surface-rooting, add mulch to the surface soil each year, as well as an acidic fertilizer. They are easy to transplant.

Camellia x *williamsii* 'Donation'

Pruning
Camellias are similar to rhododendrons: they produce a mass of blooms and do not require major pruning. If you want to train a hedge of *C. sasanqua*, plant 3 ft. (1 m) apart and regularly trim back the new growth in spring each year to encourage bushiness.

Like rhododendrons, you can remove spent blooms to promote further flowering and prevent energy going into seed production. Use pruning shears to cut back past the flowers or use your thumb and forefinger to break off spent blooms. For larger-flowering varieties, remove all but the outward-facing buds, to encourage bigger blooms. Remember that flower buds are more swollen than leaf buds.

The old adage to prune a camellia so that a bird can fly through it is useful advice. While you want a reasonably dense foliage, it is a good idea to remove some of the longer leaders to let in more light and air. This will encourage growth from lower down, improving the health and flowering of the plant. If left, plants tend to flower only at the top. Prune any time after flowering.

While camellias can be cut almost to ground level, this is not necessarily good practice. Hard pruning will create a mass of epicormic shoots or can cause dieback. This dense growth may be suitable for a hedge, but not if you want to improve flowering. To do this, thin out a lot of the growth as described above. While it may take longer to achieve improved flowering, you will get better results in the long term.

Propagation
From semi-ripe stem cuttings taken in fall.

Campsis x *tagliabuana* 'Mme Galen'

Campsis
Trumpet creeper, trumpet vine

FAMILY: Bignoniaceae

hardiness rating: 5–9

These deciduous climbers are from East Asia and North America. The name *campsis* comes from the Greek *kampe*, meaning bent, referring to the curved stamens in the flower. They are grown for their attractive trumpet flowers. The two species in this genus are *Campsis grandiflora* (syn. *Bignonia grandiflora*, *C. chinensis*, *Tecoma grandiflora*, Chinese trumpet creeper, Chinese trumpet vine) and *C. radicans* (syn. *Bignonia radicans*, *Tecoma radicans*, trumpet creeper). Plus there is a hybrid of the two, *C.* x *tagliabuana*.

They tolerate coastal winds and full sun.

Pruning
Cut back the lateral growths — the long shoots arising from the main framework — each year in spring. Cut back to two or three buds from the main stems using pruning shears. If left unpruned, they will become unruly.

Propagation
From seed, root cuttings or suckers, and stem cuttings.

Carpinus betulus

Carpinus
Hornbeam

FAMILY: Carpinaceae

hardiness rating: 4–9

These deciduous trees are from Europe, East Asia and North and Central America. They are ideal specimen trees, with attractive leaves, bark and fruit. *Carpinus betulus* (European hornbeam, hornbeam) can grow to 80 ft. (25 m), but 30 ft. (9 m) is average. *C. betulus* 'Fastigiata' (syn. 'Pyramidalis') has a narrow growth habit. *C. caroliniana* (American hornbeam, blue beech, ironwood) can grow to 40 ft. (12 m).

They prefer full sun, and tolerate heavy frosts and most soil types.

Pruning Ψ
Remove the 3 Ds, especially the deadwood in the center of the crown. You can raise the crown to expose the trunk by cutting back branches to their collar with a pruning saw. *C. betulus* can bleed sap after pruning in late winter or early spring, so even though it doesn't directly harm the tree, avoid pruning during these times.

Propagation

From seed that has been stratified for 12 weeks.

Ceanothus
California lilac

FAMILY: RHAMNACEAE

hardiness rating: 7–10

These hardy, evergreen and deciduous shrubs originate mainly from California, as the common name suggests. *Ceanothus papillosus* var. *roweanus* is commonly grown for its bright blue flowers in spring. *C. griseus* (Carmel ceanothus) and its cultivars have dark to pale blue flowers. Other species and hybrids produce flowers ranging from whites and pinks to deep purples.

Californian lilacs tolerate dry conditions, but can suffer root damage from strong winds, and die suddenly. They are difficult to transplant because they will not tolerate root disturbance.

Ceanothus griseus var. *horizontalis* 'Yankee Point'

Pruning

The ideal time to prune these plants is immediately after they flower. As they make a lot of top growth, cut them back by about one-half to nodes, using pruning shears. Pruning will keep the plant compact and less likely to suffer the root damage and dieback mentioned above. Staking is recommended for younger plants in exposed conditions.

Propagation

From soft or semi-ripe stem cuttings taken in summer and fall. Pot up as soon as rooted to avoid losses due to root disturbance.

Cedrus
Cedar

FAMILY: PINACEAE

hardiness rating: 5–9

These evergreen trees are named from the Greek word *kedros*, coniferous or cone bearing. The three main species are *Cedrus deodara* (deodar cedar) from India, *C. atlantica* (syn. *C. libani* subsp. *atlantica*, Atlas cedar) from the Atlas Mountains, and *C. libani* (cedar of Lebanon) from the Middle East. They are tall, spreading trees growing to 100 ft. (30 m). Many botanists consider that all the species of *Cedrus* are subspecies of *C. libani*.

The cedars produce valuable wood, which is fragrant. There are many different forms, including weeping, as well as different colors, including gold or blue-green. One of my favorite trees is *C. atlantica* 'Glauca' (blue Atlas cedar). The silver-blue foliage and large spreading branches make this a striking specimen tree. It will withstand dry conditions.

When buying cedars, select lightly branched specimens with a single leader. Plants that are multileadered or heavily branched will not produce the desired specimen-tree character.

Cedrus atlantica 'Glauca'

Pruning Ψ

As long as cedars are planted with plenty of space to grow, they need little pruning. Remove lower branches to improve access around the base of the tree or to let more light in. If lower branches do die back, prune back to the collar, which is very distinct. The central leader cannot be removed without ruining the shape of the tree, so make sure it can grow upward unimpeded. If two leaders develop, prune out the weaker one before it gets too big. Cedars are easily transplanted but larger trees, over 6 ft. (1.8 m), should be root pruned before moving.

C. atlantica and *C. libani* can lose branches when weighted down by snow due to their long branches being horizontal or ascending. Snow is more easily shed from branches that are descending. You can shorten the longer branches back to a suitable lateral branch as long as it doesn't spoil the shape of the tree. If branches do break, prune back to the collar.

Propagation
The green forms of cedars can be propagated from seed, but the cultivars, such as the blue Atlas cedar, are grafted.

Cercis siliquastrum

Cercis
Redbud, Judas tree
FAMILY: Caesalpinaceae

hardiness rating: 5–9

These deciduous trees and shrubs are from Europe, North America, and Eastern Asia. The name *cercis* comes from the Greek word *kerkis*, meaning weaver's shuttle, referring to the seed capsules.

They prefer full sun, shelter and regular watering during dry periods. They are grown for their attractive flowers, which appear on the bare branches in spring. Species include *Cercis canadensis* (eastern redbud), *C. chinensis* (Chinese redbud) and *C. siliquastrum* (European redbud, Judas tree).

These trees are difficult to transplant. They also benefit from staking as an aid to establishment in exposed locations.

Pruning Ψ
Remove deadwood and spindly or criss-crossing branches. If a tree gets coral spot fungus, which shows up as coral-colored spots on the leaves, prune back to healthy growth, either to a collar or lateral branch, with pruning shears or a pruning saw. If badly affected, the tree may not recover.

Propagation
From seed that has been stratified for 12 weeks, or by softwood stem cuttings.

Chaenomeles 'Toyo Nishiki'

Chaenomeles
Flowering quince
FAMILY: Rosaceae

hardiness rating: 5–9

These deciduous shrubs are from East Asia. The name *chaenomeles* comes from the Greek *chaino*, to gape, and melon, an apple, referring to the incorrect idea that the fruit is split. The colorful flowers, borne in early spring on bare branches, are their main feature. Most cultivars are hybrids of *Chaenomeles speciosa* (syn. *C. lagenaria*, *Cydonia speciosa*, *Pyrus japonica*) and *C. japonica* (syn. *C. maulei*, Japanese flowering quince, japonica).

They prefer full sun, free-draining soils and are tolerant of low temperatures.

Pruning

As with apples and pears, these plants can be trained as espaliers against a wall. Even if not espaliered, they are ideally grown against a wall to show their flowers. To contain their spreading growth habit, cut back the branches to a node with pruning shears after flowering each year.

Propagation

From seed, or from stem cuttings if a cultivar.

Chamaecyparis
False cypress

FAMILY: CUPRESSACEAE

hardiness rating: 4–9

This conifer is from Eastern Asia and North America. The name comes from the Greek *khamai*, meaning on the ground, and *kuparissos*, for cypress. Common species include *Chamaecyparis lawsoniana* (syn. *Cupressus lawsoniana*, Lawson false cypress, Port Orford cedar), which can grow to 50–80 ft. (15–25 m), and the lower-growing *C. obtusa* (syn. *Cupressus obtusa*, hinoki cypress), *C. pisifera* (syn. *Cupressus pisfera*, Sawara cypress) and *C. thyoides* (syn. *Cupressus thyoides*, white cedar, white false cypress). There are numerous cultivars of these species that are grown for their attractive foliage and diverse shapes.

They prefer free-draining soils with adequate moisture.

Chamaecyparis pisifera
'Plumosa Rogersii'

Pruning Ψ

Pruning mainly involves the removal of the 3 Ds or lifting the crown by removing lower branches. As with all conifers, avoid cutting back into old wood as it will not regenerate. If you do have to shorten branches, such as when growing *C. lawsoniana* as a hedge, do only light pruning with pruning shears to a node.

Propagation

From stem cuttings.

Chimonanthus praecox
Wintersweet

FAMILY: CALYCANTHACEAE

hardiness rating: 7–9

A deciduous shrub from China, whose name *chimonanthus* comes from the Greek *kheimon*, meaning winter, and *anthos*, flower, in reference to its time of flowering. It is best planted where the fragrant flowers can be enjoyed.

Chimonanthus praecox 'Luteus'

It grows best in full sun, with a free-draining soil and shelter from strong winds.

Pruning

As flowers develop on growth formed from the previous season, prune immediately after flowers have faded. This gives the maximum time for new wood to mature before the next winter flowering. Cut back the stems to a node past the spent flowers, using pruning shears. Cut back old or unshapely plants to near ground level with a pruning saw to promote new growth.

Propagation

From seed that has been stratified for 12 weeks.

Choisya ternata

Choisya ternata
Mexican orange blossom

FAMILY: RUTACEAE
hardiness rating: 8–10

This hardy, evergreen shrub belongs to the same family as the orange. Like many other members of this family, it has aromatic, glossy green leaves and fragrant white flowers in spring. The name *ternata* means a cluster of three, referring to the three leaflets. It is an adaptable shrub that will thrive in sun or shade, but grows much greener in the shade. It can be trained as a hedge, but is at its best when mass planted.

Pruning

Cut back after flowering to keep it bushy, although it can be left for a number of years and still maintain a tidy shape. When pruning, use pruning shears to cut back to the nearest node or use hedge clippers to give a light trim. Take off about 4 in. (10 cm) of growth.

It is susceptible to frost damage or foliage burn from hot sun and winds. Prune back past the damaged growth in both cases. However, remember that it will thrive and produce more lavish growth in shady conditions.

Propagation

From softwood and semi-ripe stem cuttings taken from spring to fall.

Cistus x *purpureus* 'Brilliancy'

Cistus
Rock rose, sun rose

FAMILY: CISTACEAE
hardiness rating: 8–10

Cistus comprises about 20 species of evergreen shrubs from the Mediterranean area. The name *cistus* is derived from a Greek word for plant. Commonly used plants are *Cistus* x *purpureus* 'Brilliancy' with deep pink flowers, and *C. salviifolius* with white flowers. The flowers are rose-like and papery in texture. Because of their Mediterranean origins, they can tolerate hot, dry conditions and infertile soils. They will grow and bloom freely and are ideal for brightening up a sunny bank.

Pruning

Cut back to the nearest node after flowering. If left, they can become untidy and leggy. Pruning can prolong their life as they otherwise tend to be short-lived. Prune back regularly to maintain compactness, as mature plants may not recover from harder pruning.

Propagation

From semi-ripe stem cuttings taken in fall.

Citrus
Citrus (lemon, lime, orange, grapefruit, etc.)

FAMILY: RUTACEAE

hardiness rating: 9–11

Citrus x *meyeri*

These evergreen shrubs and small trees are grown for their fruit. The most commonly grown is the lemon (*Citrus limon*), with *C.* x *meyeri* (syn. *C. limon* 'Meyer') also being popular. They need full sun and adequate moisture over summer and they require a minimum temperature of 37–41°F (3–5°C). Yellowing of the leaves is often due to magnesium deficiency, which can be remedied by applying Epsom salts.

Pruning

Citrus need little pruning other than removal of the 3 Ds. They flower on current season's growth. When picking the fruit, cut back to the nearest node with pruning shears. Citrus are prone to lemon tree borer so cut any infested parts back to healthy wood.

Propagation

Citrus are budded on to *Poncirus trifoliata* rootstock.

Clematis
Clematis, old man's beard, traveler's joy, virgin's bower

FAMILY: RANUNCULACEAE

hardiness rating: 4–9

Clematis x *cartmanii* 'White Carpet'

The word *clematis* is derived from the Greek *klema*, meaning vine. This climber produces a mass of beautiful flowers over a long period. The New Zealand native *Clematis paniculata* (syn. *C. terniflora*, sweet autumn clematis) produces masses of white blooms in summer, while *C. montana* 'Rubens' is a vigorous climber with pink flowers. The hybrid clematis have flowers of red, pink, blue and white. Most clematis are deciduous, with some exceptions, such as the evergreen *C. paniculata*.

Clematis grow naturally with their roots in the shady, moist forest floor and their tops in the sun. Mulch to provide a moist root area, allow the plant to climb up to the light, and it will thrive. Clematis prefer an alkaline soil, so if necessary add a handful of lime around the base of the plant. They can be trained up a trellis or pergola. *C. paniculata* can be trained up trees, but more vigorous species, such as *C. montana*, can smother the crown of a tree or cause branch failure unless controlled.

Pruning

Pruning of clematis depends on whether the plant flowers on growth formed this season or last season.

Some clematis flower later in the summer season on the current season's growth. They can be cut back to within 6–12 in. (15–30 cm) from the ground in late winter to early spring. In this group are the late-flowering hybrids such as C. 'Ville de Lyon'.

Other clematis flower earlier, for about two months during spring. They produce flowers on growth that has been formed the preceding year. They need little pruning, if at all. Examples include C. 'Barbara Jackman' and *C. montana*. The latter can be lightly trimmed for shape.

Propagation

From semi-ripe stem cuttings taken from summer to fall. Cuttings can be taken as internodal cuttings rather than the usual nodal cuttings.

Clethra

Lily-of-the-valley tree, summersweet, sweet pepperbush, white alder

FAMILY: CLETHRACEAE

hardiness rating: 3–9

The evergreen and deciduous trees and shrubs in this genus come from Asia, North America and the Madeira Islands. The name *clethra* is from the Greek *klethra*, for alder, referring to the resemblance of its leaves to that of the alder.

These plants prefer similar conditions to rhododendrons, as they are both woodland natives. They prefer cooler conditions, adequate moisture over drier periods, and a free-draining, acidic soil. They are grown for their fragrant flowers. *Clethra alnifolia* (sweet pepperbush) is deciduous and comes from the United States, while the evergreen *C. arborea* (lily-of-the-valley tree) is from the Madeira Islands. As with rhododendrons, they are prone to thrip infestation. These sap-sucking insects give the leaves a silvery appearance.

Clethra arborea

Pruning

C. alnifolia sends up suckers, and tends to produce shoots from the base of the plant. Cut back the suckers and older branches to the collar with a pruning saw. The other species can have older branches removed, as well as the 3 Ds.

Propagation

From seed, semi-ripe cuttings or suckers.

Coleonema pulchellum (syn. *C. pulchrum*)
Breath-of-heaven

FAMILY: RUTACEAE
hardiness rating: 9–10

Another member of the Rutaceae family with aromatic leaves, this evergreen South African shrub was formerly known as *Diosma*, which means breath-of-heaven. Whether or not the scent is heavenly is a matter of personal taste, but the heath-like foliage and white or pink flowers in spring are certainly attractive.

As a native of South Africa, the shrub prefers full sun and good drainage, and requires a minimum temperature of 37–41°F (3–5°C). Breath-of-heaven is ideally used for mass planting, thriving on hot, dry banks.

Pruning

If left, this shrub can become leggy, especially if it isn't in full sun. Regular pruning after flowering will keep it bushy and promote further blooms. Lightly cut back, just past the spent flowers, with hedge clippers.

Coleonema pulchellum

Using pruning shears, you can also remove some of the older stems back to a healthy lateral branch to open up the shrub and encourage new growth.

Propagation

From softwood or semi-ripe stem cuttings taken from spring to fall.

Coprosma
Coprosma

FAMILY: RUBIACEAE
hardiness rating: 8–10

These evergreen shrubs are mostly from New Zealand. The name *coprosma* comes from the Greek *kopros*, meaning dung, and *osme*, meaning smell, referring to the bad odour of the leaves of some species when crushed. Due to their diverse growth habits, they can be used as groundcovers, screens or specimens. Groundcovers include *Coprosma* x *kirkii*, while variegated shrubs include cultivars such as *C. repens* 'Marble Queen'.

Coprosma repens 'Marble Queen'

They are drought hardy, grow in sun or shade and tolerate coastal winds, but some are frost tender when young.

Pruning

The groundcovers need little pruning unless they require containing, in which case trim them back with hedge clippers. The shrubs can be pruned once or twice a year to keep them bushy and shaped. Cut back lightly with hedge clippers or to a node with pruning shears if the growth is more woody.

Propagation

From stem cuttings if a cultivar; species can be raised from seed.

Cordyline australis

Cordyline australis (syn. *Dracaena australis*)
FAMILY: Agavaceae
Cabbage tree, giant dracaena,
hardiness rating: 7–11
New Zealand cabbage palm

The cabbage tree is one of New Zealand's most distinctive plants. The name *cordyline* means club, referring to the long, tapering roots. It has very tropical-looking, sword-like leaves and a long trunk, not unlike a palm. Fragrant, white flowers appear in summer. It can grow to 20 ft. (6 m).

In New Zealand, cabbage trees grow naturally in groups in swampy areas. They are very adaptable, growing in boggy or dry areas, and apparently indifferent to climatic conditions. They can be used singly, in groups or in large containers.

Pruning Ψ

These trees need little pruning. They will naturally branch on their own after flowering, but you can make them branch out at any height by cutting through the main stem.

It is a good idea to remove the lower leaves as they die, as they can look unsightly. They are also the bane of every lawn mower! Because of their long peg-like roots, mature specimens are difficult to transplant without breaking these.

Propagation

They can be easily propagated from seed or from sections of stem set in the soil or pots.

Cornus kousa var. *chinensis*

Cornus
FAMILY: Cornaceae
Cornel, dogwood
hardiness rating: 2–8

These mostly deciduous trees and shrubs are from Asia and North America. The name *cornus* is Latin, while the common name dogwood is thought to have originated from the use of the bark mixture to bathe dogs. They are ideal specimens with their attractive flowers, bark and fruit.

They include *Cornus capitata* from the Himalayas and China, which is evergreen and grows to 27 ft. (8 m). *C. florida* (flowering dogwood) from North America is commonly grown, along with its many cultivars. It is deciduous, and can reach 13 ft. (4 m). *C. alba* 'Elegantissima' (redtwig dogwood) from Asia is a deciduous shrub with red stems, creamy white flowers and gray-green white-margined leaves. *C. kousa* (kousa dogwood) is a small deciduous Japanese tree. *C. mas* (cornelian cherry), also deciduous, can grow to 20 ft. (6 m). it bears yellow flowers in early spring and the bright red berries that follow are edible.

Dogwoods prefer free-draining, slightly acidic soils, with cool, moist conditions for their roots. They tolerate frosts, but do best if sheltered from strong, drying winds.

Pruning Ψ

C. alba can be heavily pruned each year in spring with a pruning saw. The other species and cultivars should not need pruning, other than the removal of the 3 Ds. Crown-raising is a possibility for the trees.

Propagation

From stratified seed, stem cuttings, suckers or by grafting of cultivars of C. florida.

Corylopsis
Winter hazel

FAMILY: HAMAMELIDACEAE

hardiness rating: 5–9

These deciduous shrubs come from Asia. The name *corylopsis* comes from the Greek *korylos*, hazel, and *opsis*, similar, referring to the resemblance to *Corylus*, or hazel. Like rhododendrons, they can be easily transplanted as they have fibrous roots. The yellow flowers are fragrant. Species include *Corylopsis spicata*, growing to 6 ft. (1.8 m), *C. sinensis* (syn. *C. willmottiae*), growing to 15 ft. (4.5 m), and *C. platypetala*, growing to 9 ft. (2.6 m).

Corylopsis sinensis var. *calvescens*

They prefer similar conditions to rhododendrons, camellias and pieris, that is, a sheltered location, sun or partial shade, with an acidic soil that has adequate moisture over summer.

Pruning

Little pruning is required, apart from that necessary to keep a good shape. Cut back any long shoots to a suitable node with pruning shears.

Propagation

From seed, stem cuttings in summer, and by layering.

Corylus
Filbert, hazel

FAMILY: CORYLACEAE

hardiness rating: 4–9

These deciduous nut trees come from the Northern Hemisphere. The hazel *Corylus avelluna* is a tree growing to 20 ft. (6 m), but will form a thicket of sucker growth. *C. colurna* (Turkish hazel) is a tree that can grow to 50 ft. (15 m). *C. maxima* (filbert) is similar to hazel.

They are tolerant of low temperatures and alkaline soils.

Corylus avellana 'Contorta'

Pruning Ψ

C. avellana can be cut back to ground level in winter if it becomes ungainly. C. colurna needs little pruning other than removal of the 3 Ds and any suckers. Use a pruning saw to cut these suckers back to a collar. On C. maxima, remove any weak, spindly growth back to a collar.

Propagation

From hardwood cuttings.

Cotinus coggygria

Cotinus

FAMILY: ANACARDIACEAE

Smoke bush, Venetian sumac, rhus

hardiness rating: 5–8

These deciduous shrubs and small trees are from Asia, North America and Europe. The word *kotinus* is Greek for wild olive. Its meaning is unclear. The name *coggygria* is from the Greek *kokkugia*, for the smoke bush with the gray, wispy flowers. *Cotinus coggygria* (syn. *Rhus continus*, Venetian sumac) includes a number of purple-leaved cultivars, growing to 10 ft. (3 m). *C. obovatus* (syn. *C. americanus*, *Rhus cotinoides*, American smoke tree, Chittamwood) grows to 30 ft. (9 m). The bark can cause skin irritations.

They are tolerant of a range of conditions, but will provide a better display of fall foliage and flowering with cold winters, poorer soils and dry summers.

Pruning

If grown for their foliage, cut back the plants heavily each year in winter. Cut back to the second or third-lowest node using a pruning saw or pruning shears. If grown for their flowers, the plants will need little pruning other than cutting back straggly growth to a collar or suitable lateral branch.

Propagation

From stem cuttings taken from spring to summer.

Cotoneaster integrifolius

Cotoneaster

FAMILY: ROSACEAE

Rockspray

hardiness rating: 5–9

These deciduous and evergreen shrubs and small trees are from Europe, North Africa and Asia. The name *cotoneaster* comes from the Latin *cotoneum* (quince) and *aster* (similar) referring to its similarity to quince. (It is in the same family.) The plants have attractive berries and well shaped branches.

- *Cotoneaster conspicuus* (syn. *C. conspicuus* var. *decorus*, cotoneaster, wintergreen) is an evergreen groundcover 12 in. (30 cm) high, with a wide spread.
- *C. horizontalis* (rockspray) is a deciduous groundcover with herringbone branches growing flat to the ground.
- *C. integrifolius* (syn. *C. microphyllus*) is evergreen and reaches 3 ft. (1 m).
- *C. salicifolius* (syn. *C. floccosus*) is an evergreen that grows to 16 ft. (5 m), but includes prostrate cultivars.
- *C. lacteus* is an evergreen shrub growing to 10 ft. (3 m).

Cotoneasters are reasonably frost hardy, tolerate most soils and prefer full sun. Like other members of the rose family, they can get fireblight, the bacterial disease that causes sudden dieback.

Pruning

They need little pruning other than the removal of dead or damaged wood back to a collar or node. It is important to give the plants adequate room to grow, so that the attractive branch patterns can be displayed. You can train the shrubs as hedges, but if you shorten the branches back too far you can lose flowers and fruit for the following year.

Propagation
From seed or stem cuttings taken in summer and fall.

Crataegus
Hawthorn

FAMILY: ROSACEAE

hardiness rating: 4–9

These deciduous shrubs and small trees are from the Northern Hemisphere. The name *crataegus* comes from the Greek *kratos*, for strength, referring to the strength and hardness of the wood. They flower profusely in spring and bear attractive fruits.

- *Crataegus laevigata* (syn. *C. oxyacantha*, English hawthorn) grows to 16 ft. (5 m), and includes many cultivars with attractive flowers.
- *C. monogyha* (singleseed hawthorn), which is the English hedgerow thorn, is similar.
- *C. pedicellata* grows to 16 ft. (5 m) with bright red fruit.
- *C. phaenopyrum* (syn. *C. cordata*, Washington hawthorn) from the United States grows to 30 ft. (9 m), and has white flowers and scarlet fruits.

Hawthorns grow in full or partial sun, and do well in poorer soils. They are prone to fireblight and the pear slug.

Crataegus laevigata

Pruning
Little pruning is required, unless trained as a hedge, where hedge clippers can be used once or twice a year. Cut back old, ungainly specimens to near ground level with a pruning saw to help rejuvenate them. Trees need little pruning other than removing lower branches to a collar or node if near a pathway, as the leaf spines are sharp. For the same reason, use gloves when handling the pruned branches.

Propagation
From stratified seed or stem cuttings.

Crinodendron
Lantern tree

FAMILY: ELAEOCARPACEAE

hardiness rating: 8–9

These evergreen plants come from South America. The name *crinodendron* comes from the Greek *krinon*, lily, and *dendron*, tree, in reference to their flowers. They have attractive flowers and fruit. *Crinodendron hookerianum* (syn. *Tricuspidaria lanceolata*, lantern tree) grows to 10 ft. (3 m), while *C. patagua* grows to 13 ft. (4 m).

They are frost hardy, preferring cooler summers, but require shelter from cold winds, and an acidic soil that is high in organic matter.

Crinodendron hookerianum

Pruning

Little pruning is required, other than removal of the 3 Ds. If grown as a lawn specimen, raise the crown by removing the lower branches back to the collar with a pruning saw.

Propagation

From stem cuttings taken in late spring to fall.

Cryptomeria japonica
Japanese cedar

FAMILY: Taxodiaceae

hardiness rating: 6–9

This evergreen tree hales originally from China and Japan. The name *cryptomeria* comes from the Greek *kryptos*, to hide, and *meris*, a part, referring to the concealed floral parts. The species name refers to its origin in Japan. It can be used as shelter tree, or as a specimen.

Cryptomeria japonica can grow to 36 ft. (11 m), but there is a wide range of cultivars. *C. japonica* 'Vilmoriniana' grows to 12 in. (30 cm), while the graceful *C. japonica* 'Elegans' can grow to 30 ft (9 m).

It is tolerant of most conditions.

Cryptomeria japonica 'Atawi'

Pruning Ψ

Little pruning is required other than removal of the 3 Ds. Because of their long branches, some trees may get bent to the ground under the weight of heavy rain or snow. To rectify this, you may have to remove some of the lower branches back to the collar.

Propagation

From stem cuttings taken from late summer to winter.

Cupressus
Cypress

FAMILY: Cupressaceae

hardiness rating: 6–10

These evergreen trees and shrubs originate from China, the Himalayas, North America and the Mediterranean. The name *cupressus* comes from the Greek *kuparissos*, meaning cypress tree. Grown for their strong forms, cypress are tolerant of most climatic and soil conditions. *Cupressus macrocarpa* (Monterey cypress) from California is used as a shelter tree, but is too large for surburban gardens. There are, however, many cultivars of this species that are smaller in size. *C. sempervirens* (Italian cypress, Mediterranean cypress) is the classical Italian cypress with its upright form. Cultivars include *C. sempervirens* 'Stricta', and *C. sempervirens* 'Swane's Gold'.

Cypress are prone to a fungous disease, cypress canker.

Cupressus sempervirens
'Swane's Gold'

Pruning Ψ

Little pruning is required other than the removal of the 3 Ds. Remember that conifers cannot be hard pruned to bare wood, as they will not regenerate. If you do want to clip them, then cut them back lightly with pruning shears or hedge clippers.

Cultivars of *C. sempervirens*, such as *C. sempervirens* 'Stricta', can suffer branch fallout. Often this occurs when the branches are tied with string to keep them from falling out, and the string breaks. It is better to not use string, and if any branches do start to fall out, cut them back to a node to keep the shape, or simply tuck them back in. Once large branches fall out, it is very difficult to restore the tree to a desirable shape, and the tree may need removing. Branch snapping can occur with *C. macrocarpa*, particularly after heavy pruning, as when the growth is dense the branches support each other. When opened up by thinning, they are more prone to wind damage.

Propagation
From seed and stem cuttings or by grafting.

Cytisus scoparius

Cytisus (syn. *Argyrocytisus*)
Broom

FAMILY: FABACEAE
hardiness rating: 6–9

These evergreen and deciduous shrubs come mainly from the Mediterranean. The name *cytisus* comes from the Greek *kytisos*, referring to the pea family, of which this plant is a member.

They flower prolifically. The growing conditions and pruning techniques are similar for the other brooms, *Genista* and *Spartium*.

Cytisus x *kewensis* is a low, deciduous shrub ideal for rock gardens, as is *C. procumbens*. *C.* x *praecox* grows to 4 ft. (1.2 m), and *C. multiflorus* (syn. *C. albus*) grows to 10 ft. (3 m). *C. scoparius* (Scotch broom) is the common broom with many colorful hybrids. *C. battandieri* (syn. *Argyrocytisus battandieri*, pineapple broom) grows to a tree of 13–16 ft. (4–5 m). They are very hardy, growing in full sun, in free-draining, low-fertility soils.

Pruning
The prostrate brooms require no pruning. The tree forms, such as *C. battandieri*, can have deadwood removed back to the collar. The shrubby brooms become lank and woody if left unpruned, so cut back once the flowers fade, and before the pods develop. Cut back to a node past the old flowers, using pruning shears.

Propagation
From seed soaked before sowing, or from stem cuttings taken in late summer for cultivars and hybrids .

Daphne
Daphne

FAMILY: THYMELAEACEAE
hardiness rating: 8–10

Daphnes are mostly evergreen shrubs originating from the Northern Hemisphere. Their flowers are renowned for their fragrance, making them

Daphne odora 'Leucanthe'

ideal for a front entrance or pathway. They also grow well in a container.

One of the more popular daphnes is *Daphne odora* 'Leucanthe' (winter daphne). The name *odora* refers to its scent, while *leucanthe* means 'white flower', even though the flowers are tinged with pink.

D. cneorum is a dainty 4 in. (10 cm) and *D. mezereum* (February daphne) is a deciduous shrub growing to 4 ft. (1.2 m).

Daphnes prefer semi-shade and a soil that is free-draining, but moist over the drier months. They prefer an acidic soil, so adding a soil conditioner like peat is ideal.

A lot of gardeners become concerned when the leaves turn yellow. This is due to either poor drainage or iron deficiency. The iron deficiency is called lime-induced chlorosis, because the alkaline or limey conditions tie up the iron, causing chlorosis or yellowing of the leaves. This can be remedied by adding iron chelates or flowers of sulfur, or aluminum sulfate to acidify the soil. A virus can also cause yellow mottling of the leaves and stunt growth. You can buy plants that are free of known virus, or FKV as they are called.

Pruning

Most daphnes need little pruning. However, *D. odora* 'Leucanthe' can be trained to a bushy shape. Cut back to a node when removing blooms, or wait until flowering finishes and then prune back with pruning shears to nodes.

Non-flowering stems can be used for cuttings.

Propagation

From softwood and semi-ripe stem cuttings taken from spring to fall.

Davidia involucrata

Davidia involucrata
FAMILY: Davidiaceae
Dove tree, ghost tree, handkerchief tree
hardiness rating: 6–8

This deciduous tree comes from China. As it can reach 26 ft. (7.9 m) high and 16 ft. (5 m) wide, it needs ample room to grow, and is ideally used as a specimen tree. It has showy, large white flower bracts. The cultivar *Davidia involucrata* 'Vilmoriniana' is commonly grown. It needs protection from strong wind, and grows well in the sun or partial shade.

Pruning Ψ

Little pruning is required, other than the removal of the 3 Ds.

Propagation

From seed or stem cuttings in late summer.

Desfontainea spinosa

FAMILY: LOGANIACEAE
hardiness rating: 8–10

The only species in its genus, this is evergreen shrub from Peru and Chile. It is named after Rene Desfontaines, a French botanist. It has spiny leaves like holly, hence the specific name, *spinosa*, and showy, trumpet-shaped flowers. It prefers a moist, acidic soil high in organic matter. Although it tolerates light frosts, in cooler climates plant it against a sunny wall away from cold winds. In warmer climates, plant in the semi-shade away from the hot midday sun.

Desfontainea spinosa

Pruning
Little pruning is required other than removal of the 3 Ds. When removing branches, wear gloves to protect against the spiny leaves.

Propagation
From seed or stem cuttings.

Deutzia
Deutzia

FAMILY: HYDRANGEACEAE
hardiness rating: 5–8

These hardy, deciduous shrubs from Asia are ideal for a perennial border among spring-flowering bulbs. There is a variety of species and cultivars to choose from, with a spectacular range of flower color. They tolerate a wide range of soils and other conditions.

Deutzia crenata var. *nakaiana* 'Nikko'

Pruning
Prune to maintain a good shape, as the branches tend to be long and spindly. Prune after flowering or when cutting blooms. Cut back to a node past the spent flowers.

Deutzias flower on growth laid down the previous year. Older plants can be rejuvenated by cutting back to ground level flowered shoots that are two or more years old. By removing these older shoots as well as the pruning described above, you can encourage new flowering wood and maintain a compact shrub.

Propagation
From stem cuttings. Take semi-ripe cuttings in fall, or larger hardwood cuttings in winter.

Diospyros
Persimmon

FAMILY: EBENACEAE
hardiness rating: 4–10

There are about 200 species of evergreen and deciduous trees and shrubs in this genus. The name *diospyros* comes from the Greek *dios*, divine, and *puros*, grain, in reference to the edible fruits. The ebony tree is related to the persimmon.

Diospyros lotus

Persimmons are grown for their ornamental value as well as fruit. *Diospyros kaki* (Chinese persimmon, Japanese persimmon, kaki) is a deciduous tree with tasty fruit and can grow to 40 ft. (12 m). *D. lotus* (date plum) is a deciduous tree that can reach 30 ft. (9 m), but the fruit is inedible. *D. virginiana* (American persimmon, possumwood) is a deciduous tree that can grow to 60 ft. (18 m) with much favored fruit. All have spectacular fall leaf color.

Persimmon are frost tender when young but become frost hardy after two or three years.

Pruning Ψ

Little pruning is required other than removing deadwood back to the collar with a pruning saw. *D. virginiana* can be crown-raised by removing the lower branches to a height of 6 ft. (1.8 m).

Propagation

From stratified seed and root cuttings or by budding or grafting on to rootstock for the varieties of *D. kaki*.

Dodonaea viscosa 'Purpurea'

Dodonaea viscosa
Akeake, hop bush

FAMILY: SAPINDACEAE

hardiness rating: 8–10

This evergreen shrub is native to New Zealand. The Maori name *akeake* means everlasting, in reference to the hard, durable wood, while the specific name *viscosa* refers to the sticky or viscid leaves.

It is ideal as a hedge, tolerates harsh climatic conditions and grows just about anywhere as long as it has good drainage. Akeakes do not like being transplanted, especially if over about 12 in. (30 cm).

Pruning

If training as a hedge, plant between 3–5 ft. (1–1.5 m) apart. Each year cut back with hedge clippers. Remove about 4 in. (10 cm) of the top growth and lightly trim the sides. They can be kept to a height of about 6–8 ft. (1.8–2.4 m). If growing this plant as a shrub, remove deadwood and maintain at a desirable shape and size.

Don't prune back beyond the current year's growth as you risk dieback. Regular pruning will maintain bushiness as the plants are spindly by nature.

Propagation

From seed, including the purple-leaved form, as this comes reasonably true from seed.

Drimys winteri (syn. *Wintera aromatica*)
FAMILY: WINTERACEAE
Winter's bark
hardiness rating: 8–10

This vigorous evergreen tree is from Central and South America. The name *drimys* comes from *drimus*, meaning acrid, in reference to the taste of the bark. It grows 23–26 ft. (7–8 m), and has white, jasmine-scented flowers. Ideal as a specimen tree, it requires a moist soil, tolerates frost and wind, but prefers a warm aspect.

Pruning Ψ
Little pruning is required other than removal of the 3 Ds.

Propagation
From stem cuttings taken late spring to late fall.

Drimys winteri

Embothrium coccineum
FAMILY: PROTEACEAE
Chilean firebush, flame flower
hardiness rating: 8–10

This evergreen small tree from the Chilean Andes is the main species of the genus grown. The name *embothrium* comes from the Greek, *en*, meaning in and *bothrion*, a little pit, in reference to the anthers. The name firebush alludes to the brilliant orange-scarlet flowers. *Embothrium coccineum* 'Longifolium' is a distinct form that is superior.

The trees are native to cool, shady valleys in the Andes mountains, so prefer a moist, acidic soil. As for other members of the protea family, adding lime or fertilizer will cause sudden death.

Pruning
Little pruning is required. As with other members of the protea family, it will not regenerate if you cut it back hard.

Propagation
From seed, or from stem cuttings taken during the warmer months.

Embothrium coccineum

Erica
FAMILY: ERICACEAE
Heath, heather
hardiness rating: 7–10

These colorful, evergreen shrubs originate mostly from South Africa, the remaining ones from Europe. They have needle-like leaves and a wide range of flower color.

Ericas need full sun with acidic, free-draining soil. Like all plants that prefer acidic soil, you can add materials like peat and acidic fertilizers to maintain the correct soil conditions. Adding lime can be fatal to these plants. The South African plants are less tolerant of the cold than the European ones.

Erica vagans 'Mrs D.F. Maxwell'

They are ideal in a mass planting or mixed with other acid-loving plants.

67

Pruning

Ericas can be pruned to preserve shape and stimulate new growth and flowering. Never cut back into old wood, as it will not regenerate. Prune only past the spent flower and not to bare stems. Use pruning shears for smaller plants or hedge clippers for larger ones.

Prune summer-flowering varieties the following spring, and prune back winter-blooming plants past the flower immediately the display is over.

Propagation

From stem cuttings taken from spring to fall, or from stems which naturally layer themselves. Cut off these rooted plants and pot them in a mix without lime in it.

Eriobotrya japonica

Eriobotrya japonica
Loquat

FAMILY: Rosaceae

hardiness rating: 8–10

This evergreen tree from East Asia has attractive foliage, as well as edible fruits. The name *eriobotrya* comes from the Greek, *erion*, wool, and *botrus*, a cluster, referring to the woolly young shoots. The tree prefers full sun and a warm climate for adequate fruiting.

Pruning

Cut back older wood with a pruning saw to a collar after fruiting in spring, as this will encourage new growth from the base. If grown for ornamental use, it can be left unpruned.

Propagation

From seed, or propagated by grafting in the case of the cultivated varieties.

Eriostemon myoporoides 'Profusion'

Eriostemon myoporoides
Long-leaf waxflower

FAMILY: Rutaceae

hardiness rating: 10

These evergreen shrubs, with their starry white flowers and scented leaves, are from Australia. The name *eriostemon* comes from the Greek *erion*, wool, and *stemon*, a stamen, referring to the woolly stamens. The specific name *myoporoides* refers to the leaves resembling *Myoporum.* There are a number of cultivars, such as *Eriostemon myoporoides* 'Profusion'.

They are drought resistant, and tolerate light frosts. Grow them in a slightly acidic, free-draining soil in full sun or partial shade.

They are prone to sooty mold, which causes blackening on the leaves and stems. The sooty mold grows on honeydew secreted by sap-sucking insects found on the foliage from time to time.

Pruning

They can be cut back after flowering by about one-third. Cut back to past the flowers, using hedge clippers. This will encourage denser growth and better flowering.

Propagation
From stem cuttings.

Erythrina
Coral tree

FAMILY: FABACEAE
hardiness rating: 8–10

Erythrina crista-galli

In this genus of mostly deciduous tropical trees and shrubs are some more hardy specimens from South Africa. The name *erythrina* comes from the Greek word *erythros* for red, referring to the bright red flowers. *Erythrina crista-galli* (cock's comb, common coral tree) will die back to almost ground level in colder climates, and grow 7–10 ft. (2.1–3 m) in spring. In warmer, frost-free climates it will become a multibranched tree to 20 ft. (6 m). The new growth has spines on it. *E.* 'Blakei' is a hybrid growing to 9 ft. (2.6 m), while *E.* x *sykesii* is a hybrid growing to 20 ft. (6 m).

Grow in moist but free-draining soil in a sunny position.

Pruning
E. crista-galli can have up to three blooms per year. After flowering, cut back the old flower stems and dead branch ends using pruning shears, and wear gloves to protect your hands from the spines.

As the stems are rather fragile, branches can break in the wind. If this occurs, cut back the damaged branches to a collar.

In colder climates, the roots of *E. crista-galli* can be covered in straw or similar material to reduce the likelihood of freezing. *E.* 'Blakei' can be cut back almost to ground level after the first frost.

Propagation
From seed that has been soaked or scarified before sowing.

Escallonia
Escallonia

FAMILY: SAXIFRAGACEAE
hardiness rating: 7–9

These evergreen shrubs are from South America. They are named after Señor Escallon, a Spanish traveller. *Escallonia macrantha* is the common escallonia, while there are many hybrid cultivars such as *E.* 'Field's Scarlet', and *E.* 'Apple Blossom' They bloom for long periods over spring and summer, and are often used as hedges.

They are moderately frost hardy, will grow in most soils, sun or partial shade and tolerate salt winds.

Pruning
If growing as a hedge, use hedge clippers to trim the hedge into the desired

Escallonia 'Apple Blossom'

69

shape after flowering. You may lose the flowers with regular trimming. Shrubs can have the growing tips removed, either with pruning shears or hedge clippers. Rejuvenate old plants by cutting back the plant almost to ground level with a pruning saw.

In areas with heavy frosts, they will regenerate quickly after dying back after the frosts.

Propagation
From stem cuttings.

Eucalyptus leucoxylon 'Rosea'

Eucalyptus
Gum, ironbark

FAMILY: MYRTACEAE

hardiness rating: 8–10

This genus is a very large one with at least 600 species, mostly from Australia. The name *eucalyptus* means well-covered, referring to the cup-like covering on the flower.

Gums include some of the largest trees in the world. They have scented leaves, beautiful flowers and attractive bark. They are grown commercially for timber and as ornamentals. Common examples of the latter include:

- *Eucalyptus cinerea* (Argyle apple, silver dollar gum), with disc-shaped silver leaves.
- *E. nicholii* (narrow-leaved black peppermint, willow peppermint) with willow-like leaves.
- *E. ficifolia* (red-flowering gum) has bright red flowers.
- *E. leucoxylon* (blue gum, white ironbark, yellow gum) has cream or pink flowers.
- *E. sideroxylon* 'Rosea' (mugga, red ironbark) has pink flowers.

These plants grow rapidly in the right location. They prefer full sun and good drainage. It is essential that you consider the eventual height of each tree when planting in city areas. All too often they have to be removed because they have outgrown their space. Some species like *E. nicholii* and *E. ficifolia* are susceptible to branch and stem failure on exposed sites.

Pruning Ψ
Gums should need little pruning other than deadwooding and removing damaged limbs. As long as the height of the tree is allowed for when planting, they can be left to themselves, as they are largely self-pruning.

If the trunks are cut back hard, they will produce epicormic shoots. This spindly, dense growth (see Introduction) is weak and dieback can result if branches are cut back in this way.

The crown can be raised to improve light and access around the base. This is done by cutting back selected branches to a collar or lateral branch.

Propagation
From the abundant seed produced from the woody capsules.

Euphorbia
Milkweed, spurge, poinsettia

FAMILY: EUPHORBIACEAE

hardiness rating: 4–10

These evergreen shrubs and herbaceous perennials are mainly from Africa and Southeast Asia. *Euphorbia* is named after Euphorbus, a physician from Mauritania. The plants all have a milky-white latex in their stems. Some of the species are succulent. *Euphorbia characias* subsp. *wulfenii* (syn. *E. veneta*, *E. wulfenii*) is a hardy plant from the Balkans, growing to 3 ft. (1 m). *E. pulcherrima* (Mexican flame leaf, poinsettia) is a commonly grown herbaceous species, but generally as an indoor container plant.

They are drought hardy, and prefer full sun and a frost-free location.

Euphorbia characias

Pruning

For spurges such as *E. characias*, cut back the stems with spent flowers to the ground with pruning shears. New shoots will arise in their place. If you cut the stems back partially, they won't regenerate. When you cut stems, latex will drip from the cut, but it will dry quickly.

For poinsettias, such as *E. pulcherrima*, prune back to 8 in. (20 cm) when the colorful bracts fade in early spring. In summer, remove the tips with pruning shears to maintain bushiness.

Propagation

From seed or stem cuttings.

Euryops pectinatus
Gray-leafed europs

FAMILY: ASTERACEAE

hardiness rating: 9–10

The name *euryops* means wide eyes and refers to the large flowers. This evergreen shrub from South Africa has attractive yellow flowers and gray leaves in spring and fall. It is one of the larger daisies, reaching over 3 ft. (1 m) in height. Like nearly all daisies, euryops need full sun and good drainage. They are drought-resistant once established and suitable for mass plantings or for mixed planting.

Euryops pectinatus

Pruning

As with most daisies, euryops need to be cut back after flowering to keep them compact and to encourage further blooms. I have seen some grand old specimens that had become very woody at the base but still flowered well as a result of regular pruning.

Cut them back between one-third to one-half after flowering. Cut back to a node using pruning shears or clip back with hedge clippers to the required height.

Propagation

From stem cuttings taken at any time. They root easily, usually within two to three weeks.

Fagus sylvatica 'Purpurea'

Fagus
Beech

FAMILY: FAGACEAE
hardiness rating: 3–9

This genus of deciduous trees include 10 species from Asia and Europe. The name *fagus* comes from the Greek and Latin word for beech. They are excellent specimen trees, as long as they have adequate room to grow, but can be trained as a hedge.

Fagus sylvatica (European beech) from Britain can grow to 100 ft. (30 m). There are many cultivars of this species, including *F. sylvatica* 'Purpurea' and the weeping *F. sylvatica* 'Pendula'. *F. grandiflora* (syn. *F. americana*, American beech) from East North America can grow to 30 ft. (9 m).

Beeches are frost hardy, but need protection from strong winds, which will distort their distinctive form, or coastal winds, which will burn the foliage. They need free-draining soils, resenting wet and heavy clay soils.

Pruning Ψ
Little pruning is required other than removal of deadwood. The main thing is to provide the right growing conditions; that is, shelter from strong winds, which distort growth, and adequate room for the tree to grow unimpeded. If grown as a hedge, they need to be trained from planting. Trim the sides and top with hedge clippers each year during the growing season.

Propagation
From stratified seed, or by grafting for the cultivars of *F. sylvatica*.

Feijoa sellowiana

Feijoa sellowiana
Feijoa, pineapple guava

FAMILY: MYRTACEAE
hardiness rating: 9–11

This shrub from Brazil has ornamental as well as a commercial value as a winter fruit crop. It is in the same family as the gums, with similar colorful flowers and leaves that are resistant to drought. Feijoas make an ideal hedge as well as a specimen shrub. If using as a fruiting plant, plant in groups to get pollination, although there are cultivars that are self-fertile.

They grow well in coastal areas as well as cold inland areas, but need good drainage. Regular watering over dry periods helps fruit production.

Pruning
Like kiwifruit, feijoas fruit on the current season's growth. For fruiting plants, cut back to a node past the fruiting wood with pruning shears to encourage new growth.

For hedges, keep the plant trimmed as you would normally for a hedge. However, this may mean you do not get flowers or fruit. Trim both the sides and top with hedge clippers during the growing season. Feijoas can be trained to about 6 ft. (1.8 m) in height. For ornamental specimens, the plant can be left except for the removal of the 3 Ds.

Propagation

From softwood or semi-ripe stem cuttings taken from spring to fall. They can take months to root.

Felicia amelloides (syn. *Aster amelloides, A. capensis, A. coelestis*)
Blue daisy, blue marguerite

FAMILY: ASTERACEAE
hardiness rating: 9–11

This shrub with its blue daisy flowers is from South Africa. It is named after Felix, a 19th-century German official. The bush flowers consistently over spring and summer. There are a number of cultivars with pink or white flowers, also *Felicia amelloides* 'Santa Anita', which has larger and deeper blue flowers.

They need full sun, with a free-draining soil with adequate moisture over summer. Minimum temperature requirements are 37–41°F (3–5°C).

Felicia amelloides

Pruning

As with other daisies, their life and flowering is prolonged with pruning after flowering in late summer. Using hedge clippers, cut them back about one-half. During the flowering season deadhead as the old flower heads die off, and cut back any straggly shoots to a node, using pruning shears.

Propagation

From seed, or the cultivars from stem cuttings taken at any time.

Ficus pumila (syn. *F. repens*)
Climbing fig, creeping fig

FAMILY: MORACEAE
hardiness rating: 8–11

This evergreen climber from China and Japan bears little resemblance to other ficus species. It clings very strongly to surfaces such as brick or wood by suckers. It has both juvenile and adult foliage. The juvenile foliage has heart-shaped leaves about 1 in. (2.5 cm) long, while the adult leaves are thicker and glossier, and about 4 in. (10 cm) long. There is a smaller form, *F. pumila* 'Minima' that is preferable for smaller areas.

Creeping figs are ideal for training up walls and perform best on those walls enjoying cooler aspects.

Ficus pumila 'Quercifolia'

Pruning

Annual trimming will help to maintain the juvenile growth. This growth is more desirable as it is lighter and clings tightly to the wall. If left to itself, it can get too heavy and come away from its support. I have seen a very large section peel off from a wall due to excess weight.

Trimming once a year, using hedge clippers, will help to prevent this. Trim back as close to the wall as you can, removing outward growth. Also remove growth that grows over the top of the wall as the wind can put pressure on the remaining plant, causing it to come away.

Propagation

From softwood and semi-ripe stem cuttings taken from spring to fall.

Forsythia x intermedia 'Karl Sax'

Forsythia x *intermedia*
Forsythia

FAMILY: OLEACEAE

hardiness rating: 6–9

The parents of this deciduous shrub (*Forsythia suspensa* and *F. viridissima*) are from China. Its bright yellow flowers on bare branches are a spectacular sight in spring and the yellow works well with blue-flowering shrubs such as *Ceanothus* or spring-flowering bulbs such as daffodils.

Various cultivars of this hybrid are popular, such as *F.* x *intermedia* 'Spectabilis', a vigorous grower with deep yellow flowers.

This hardy shrub prefers cooler conditions found inland, with full sun and good drainage.

Pruning

Forsythias flower in spring, having taken a full year to reach full bloom. They should be pruned immediately after flowering because if you prune in winter, you will remove flower buds that are due to flower in spring. There is always a temptation to prune deciduous shrubs when they are without leaf, but the golden rule of pruning after flowering applies.

Remove the oldest stems to ground level with pruning shears or loppers to encourage new stems. As a general rule don't remove more than one-third of the older growth. Older plants left unpruned will have a lot of thick, old stems.

Cut back newer-flowering stems to a node when cutting flowers as this will keep the plant compact. Any deadwood should be removed.

Propagation

From stem cuttings in summer or fall, or from longer hardwood stem cuttings taken in winter. Take 4 in. (10 cm) cuttings which have been severed below a node, and plant in a free-draining mix outdoors.

Fraxinus excelsior 'Pendula'

Fraxinus
Ash

FAMILY: OLEACEAE

hardiness rating: 5–9

Deciduous trees in this genus are native to cooler Northern Hemisphere countries. *Fraxinus* comes from the Latin word for ash. *Excelsior* means tall; these trees need room to grow unimpeded as they can reach 120 ft. (36 m).

Ashes make spectacular specimen trees, with their attractive form and colorful leaves. *Fraxinus excelsior* 'Aurea' (European ash) has yellow leaves with black buds, while *F. angustifolia* 'Raywood' (Caucasian ash, claret ash) has spectacular claret-red leaves in fall.

They can tolerate wet conditions, but strong winds can burn foliage and cause structural damage to branches.

Pruning Ψ

These trees need little regular pruning as long as they are planted in the correct location. As with all trees, they need deadwooding. You can raise the crown to give better access around the tree as the branches can droop. Use a pruning saw, making sure you undercut branches. Cut to the branch collar or shorten back to a lateral branch.

Propagation

Species of ash such as *F. excelsior* can be propagated from seed, but the cultivars are budded or grafted on to a rootstock.

Fremontodendron (syn. *Fremontia*)
Flannel bush

FAMILY: STERCULIACEAE
hardiness rating: 8–10

Named after John Freemont, an American explorer, this genus includes two species from California and Mexico. Both shrubs are evergreen in warm areas and semi-deciduous in colder climates. They have maple-like foliage and showy golden-yellow flowers produced over a long period.

The two species are *Fremontodendron californicum* (California flannel bush) and *F. mexicanum* (Mexican flannel bush). *F.* 'California Glory' is a cross between the two species.

Flannel bushes tolerate heavy frosts and droughts. Plant in a free-draining, slightly alkaline soil. They may require staking.

Fremontodendron mexicanum

Pruning Ψ

They need little more than removal of dead or damaged branches back to the collar, using a pruning saw. The small trees can become top heavy and prone to damage to the roots as a result of the wind rocking them. Initial staking will help limit this possibility. Reducing the amount of top growth will also help lessen the likelihood of the plant toppling over.

Propagation

From seed that has been soaked or scarified.

Fuchsia
Fuchsia

FAMILY: ONAGRACEAE
hardiness rating: 7–11

This large genus, with thousands of popular cultivars, includes around 100 species from Central and South America, and New Zealand. Fuchsias can be used in hanging baskets and other containers, trained as standards or planted in groups. There is even a groundcover, *Fuchsia procumbens* (trailing fuchsia), which can be used in rock gardens in mild climates.

Fuchsias prefer cool, shady conditions away from drying winds and hot sun. They need regular watering and feeding. Mulching and overhead watering will help to maintain good health. Their attractive flowers can bloom for up to six months.

Fuchsia paniculata

75

Pruning

As fuchsias flower on new growth, pruning will encourage flowering. For standards, hanging baskets and containers, keep taking out the tips as the plant grows in order to get dense growth. Use pruning shears or your thumb and forefinger to pinch out the soft growth. Once the plant finishes flowering, cut back past the flowers to a node. The same applies to shrubs planted out in the garden.

Older shrubs will become leggy if left unpruned. Cut them back to a manageable size using a pruning saw. Fuchsias will respond to hard pruning and produce a mass of new growth.

Propagation

From softwood and semi-ripe stem cuttings taken from spring to fall.

Gardenia augusta 'Radicans'

Gardenia augusta
Cape jasmine, common gardenia

FAMILY: RUBIACEAE
hardiness rating: 8–10

This medium to large evergreen shrub from Asia has glossy leaves and very fragrant white blooms in spring and summer. Many popular cultivars have been developed from this species. Because of its tropical origins, grow this plant in a warm, sheltered location outdoors, or indoors in a pot.

Gardenias, like daphnes, prefer acidic soil. Plant in a material such as peat, and keep moist in summer by regular watering and misting of the leaves. Also, as with daphne, they get chlorosis of the leaves, which can be corrected with sulfate of iron.

Pruning

Gardenias should be cut back after flowering to keep them compact and flowering well. Cut back to a node, past the flower, when the blooms are spent. Older plants can be cut almost to ground level to rejuvenate them.

Propagation

From stem cuttings taken at any time of the year.

Garrya elliptica 'James Roof'

Garrya elliptica
Silk-tassel bush, tassel tree

FAMILY: GARRYACEAE
hardiness rating: 8–10

This is an evergreen shrub from the coasts of Oregon and California. Named after Nicholas Garry, a 19th-century explorer, it is grown for the attractive flowers borne in spring. These catkins are found on the commonly grown male plant. *Garrya elliptica* 'James Roof' is an improved form, with silvery, gray-green catkins.

This shrub grows to around 12 ft. (3.6 m) in sun or partial shade, and tolerates coastal winds and drought.

Pruning

Little pruning of these shrubs is required. Spindly growth can be shortened back to a node after the flowers fade. Use pruning shears.

Propagation

The more desirable form is propagated from stem cuttings.

Gaultheria (syn. x *Gaulnettya, Pernettya*)
Snowberry, wintergreen

FAMILY: ERICACEAE

hardiness rating: 3–9

These low-growing evergreen shrubs come from North America, the West Indies and Japan through to Australasia. They are named after Jean Gaultier, a French botanist. As with many other members of the Ericaceae family, they prefer shade or semi-shade, and moisture-retentive, lime-free, acidic soils high in organic matter. They are valued for their foliage, fragrant flowers and fleshy fruits.

Cultivated species include *Gaultheria cuneata* and *G. miqueliana*, both reaching 12 in. (30 cm), with white flowers and fruit. *G. mucronata* (syn. *Pernettya mucronata*) grows to 24 in. (60 cm). *G. procumbens* (checkerberry, wintergreen) has strongly fragrant leaves and grows to only 12 in. (30 cm). *G. shallon* (salal, shallon) grows to 6 ft. (1.8 m), with pink-white flowers in spring and summer.

Gaultheria mucronata
'Bell's Seedling'

Pruning

These shrubs don't need regular pruning, but can be shaped to keep them compact. Using pruning shears, cut back to suitable nodes after flowering.

Propagation

From seed, stem cuttings or from layers.

Gaura lindheimeri
White gaura

FAMILY: ONAGRACEAE

hardiness rating: 6–9

These clump-forming herbaceous perennials from the Texas-Mexico area grow to 4 ft. (1.2 m). From early summer to fall they bear long panicles of butterfly-like white flowers that fade pink. They prefer full sun and a free-draining soil.

Gaura lindheimeri

Pruning

Cut to the ground after flowering, using pruning shears.

Propagation

From seed sown in spring or fall, or stem cuttings taken in summer.

Gelsemium sempervirens

Gelsemium sempervirens
Carolina jasmine, Carolina yellow jessamine

FAMILY: LOGANIACEAE

hardiness rating: 7–9

This evergreen climber is from the Southeastern United States. Its yellow blossom is the state flower of South Carolina. The name *gelsemium* comes from the Latin *gelsomino*, a jasmine, referring to the jasmine-like, fragrant, yellow flowers, although it is not related to jasmine. The perennial has a twining growth habit and reaches 10 ft. (3 m).

It grows in sun or partial shade in a free-draining soil.

Pruning
This plant can be used as a groundcover or trained on fences, pergolas or walls, preferably near an entrance so that the perfume can be enjoyed. It will need fixing to these structures at an early stage. Cut back after flowering to keep the plant compact, using hedge clippers.

Propagation
From seed or stem cuttings.

Gingko biloba

Ginkgo biloba
Maidenhair tree

FAMILY: GINKGOACEAE

hardiness rating: 5–9

This deciduous tree was originally known only from pollen fossil records until it was discovered growing near remote Chinese temples. It is the only species in this ancient family. Ginkgo is a Chinese name, while the common name maidenhair refers to the leaves' resemblance to the maidenhair fern.

It makes an attractive specimen tree up to 80 ft. (25 m), with spreading branches and good fall color. It is especially useful in city areas as it is pollution-resistant. There are both male and female plants, but the female is less desirable as an amenity tree because of its smelly fruit.

Pruning Ψ
Ginkgos need training at an early stage to maintain a straight trunk. If the site is exposed, stake the tree, but the stake should support only between one-half to one-third of the height of the tree. It helps to support the roots until they are established.

They need little pruning other than removal of the 3 Ds. They have a tendency to form more than one leader so remove the weaker competing ones back to the collar at an early stage.

Propagation
From seed, but the various cultivars are grafted.

Gleditsia triacanthos
Honey locust

FAMILY: FABACEAE
hardiness rating: 3–7

This thorny, deciduous tree is from North America. The genus is named after J. Gleditch, from the Berlin Botanic Gardens, while the species name *triacanthos* means armed with sharp thorns. *Gleditsia triacanthos* can grow to 100 ft. (30 m) in its native habitat, but is seldom grown as a specimen tree because of its thorns. It has fruit pods 12 in. (30 cm) long. *G. tricanthos* f. *inermis* is almost completely free of thorns, as are most of the modern cultivars, including the golden-leafed 'Sunburst', and 'Rubylace', with bronzy red foliage.

Gleditsia triacanthos 'Sunburst'

The honey locust is tolerant of a range of conditions. These trees are very drought hardy, but strong winds can cause structural damage to their branches.

Pruning Ψ
If planted as a specimen tree with adequate room, gleditsia needs little pruning other than the removal of dead or damaged branches. Due to their spreading habit and the length of their branches, trees may need to be crown-raised or have the longer branches shortened back to a suitable lateral branch. If raising the crown, cut back to a collar, using a pruning saw. If pruning trees with thorns, use gloves.

Propagation
Cultivars are grafted on to seedling rootstocks.

Gordonia axillaris

FAMILY: THEACEAE
hardiness rating: 9–10

This evergreen species is the main one of the genus grown, and is native to China, Taiwan and Vietnam. It is named after James Gordon, an 18th-century English nurseryman. It is in the camellia or tea family, being similar in appearance, and requires the same growing conditions. It grows to 30 ft. (9 m), and has creamy-white flowers from fall to spring.

It prefers sun or partial shade, shelter, and organically rich, slightly acidic soils that are moisture-retentive.

Pruning
Little pruning is required other than removal of the 3 Ds.

Gordonia axillaris

Propagation
From seed or stem cuttings.

Griselinia littoralis 'Broadway Mint'

Griselinia
Broadleaf, kapuka, puka

FAMILY: CORNACEAE

hardiness rating: 8–9

The two New Zealand species in this genus are handsome foliage trees growing up to 20 ft. (6 m). *Griselinia littoralis* (broadleaf, kapuka) grows in coastal locations in New Zealand, hence its name *littoralis*, which means shore-growing. *G. lucida* (puka) grows in the forest, and the name *lucida* refers to its glossy leaves. It will grow in soil even though it naturally grows perched in trees, where it sends down its roots to the soil. There is a variegated cultivar of *G. littoralis*.

G. littoralis is tolerant of coastal conditions. Both plants need good drainage. They are ideal as specimen trees, hedges, background planting or as container plants.

Pruning Ψ
These trees need little pruning other than removal of the 3 Ds. They can be crown-raised to improve light and access under the tree. If using as a screen, plant them closer together and keep the sides pruned back to suitable lateral branches.

Propagation
From stem cuttings taken at any time of the year.

Hakea prostrata

Hakea
Hakea

FAMILY: PROTEACEAE

hardiness rating: 9–11

The evergreen shrubs and small trees in this genus are all from Australia. The name *hakea* comes from Baron von Hake, a German patron of botany. *Hakea laurina* (pincushion bush) has rosy red flowers and grows to 20 ft. (6 m). *H. salicifolia* 'Gold Medal' (willow-leaved hakea) has yellow-variegated leaves.

Hakeas need full sun, and a well-drained, acidic soil. They are ideal coastal plants.

Pruning
As with most members of the Proteaceae family, you can prune back to a node past the spent flowers or when picking the flowers, but if you prune back into old wood, hakeas won't regenerate. Pruning after flowering will produce a more bushy plant and encourage further flowering. Old plants that have been left unpruned can get very woody and leggy, especially if in a shady position. Once they get like this, you can't regenerate them by hard pruning, so it is better to replace the plants.

Propagation
From seed that has been soaked or scarified, or by stem cuttings.

Halesia
Silverbell, snowdrop tree

FAMILY: Styracaeae

hardiness rating: 5–9

These deciduous trees are from Southeastern United States and China. They are named after Stephen Hales, an author. They are tolerant of most climatic conditions, but don't like lime, and resent a windy, exposed position. They have snowdrop-like white flowers. The two main species in cultivation are *Halesia carolina* (syn. *H. tetraptera*, Carolina silverbell), growing to 12 ft. (3.6 m), and *H. monticola* (mountain silverbell), which reaches 50 ft. (15 m).

Halesia carolina

Pruning Ψ

No regular pruning is required. *H. carolina* is naturally thickly branched, and no thinning-out is necessary. Cut back to a node past the spent flowers to contain its size and keep it compact.

Propagation

From stratified seed sown in spring.

Hamamelis
Witch hazel

FAMILY: Hamamelidaceae

hardiness rating: 3–8

These hardy, deciduous shrubs are from North America and East Asia. The name *hamamelis* is Greek for a pear-shaped fruit. The common name refers to its resemblance to hazel. The three main species grown are: *Hamamelis mollis* (Chinese witch hazel), which reaches 12 ft. (3.6 m) and includes a number of cultivars; *H.* x *intermedia*, which grows to 10 ft. (3 m); and *H. virginiana* (common witch hazel) which grows to 13 ft. (4 m). All shrubs have fragrant, yellow flowers, except *H. mollis* and its cultivars, whose blossoms include dark red, coppery orange and gold colors.

Witch hazels are very tolerant of cold, and prefer a moisture-retentive, free-draining soil that is slightly acidic. Plant in full sun or partial shade, and protect from cold or drying winds. Check for scale insects, and spray with an oil-based insecticide as needed.

Hamamelis x *intermedia* 'Jelena'

Pruning

Little pruning is required other than keeping the plant compact, and reducing side shoots. Cut back branches to a collar or node with pruning shears, during the period after flowering and before the leaves appear.

Propagation

From stratified seed, or from stem cuttings taken from cultivars during summer to fall.

Hardenbergia
Coral pea

FAMILY: Fabaceae

hardiness rating: 10–11

These evergreen climbers from Australia are vigorous plants with masses

81

Hardenbergia violacea 'Alba'

of pea-shaped flowers in late winter to spring. The one most commonly grown is *Hardenbergia violacea* (syn. *H. monophylla*, purple coral pea) or one of its cultivars, such as *H. violacea* 'Happy Wanderer' with purple-blue flowers.

They tolerate coastal conditions and will scramble easily over banks. They can be trained up structures, but their tendrils need to be tied. They can be damaged by caterpillars, so keep an eye out for holes in the leaves and apply an appropriate insecticide if damage is other than cosmetic.

Pruning

These climbers are very hardy and will tolerate severe pruning. If left unpruned, they can become untidy. Prune back almost to ground level after flowering. You can do this once every two years or as the plant's shape dictates.

Propagation

From stem cuttings cut below the node. They can be taken from spring to fall. Roots should form after about a month.

Hebe subalpina

Hebe
Hebe

FAMILY: Scrophulariaceae

hardiness rating: 8–11

These evergreen shrubs are found almost exclusively in New Zealand. The name *hebe* is derived from the Goddess of Youth. The range of hebes is enormous, the flowers being the main feature of the cultivated forms.

The alpine hebes, like the whipcords, have unusual foliage, while the many cultivars are grown for their flowers. The cultivars are very adaptable, tolerating most conditions, including coastal. They are ideal for planting in groups in a garden of New Zealand natives, while the alpine hebes are ideal for a rock garden.

Pruning

The flowering hebes need regular pruning after flowering to keep them compact and to promote more blooms. They flower on new growth. If left unpruned, hebes will become straggly and flower only at the tips. Hard pruning at this stage can cause dieback.

Once the flowers have faded, cut back to a node past the flowers, using either pruning shears or hedge clippers. Do this at least once a year. The whipcord hebes do not need pruning other than shaping.

Propagation

From softwood and semi-ripe stem cuttings taken in spring and fall.

Hedera
Ivy

FAMILY: ARALIACEAE

hardiness rating: 5–11

These evergreen climbing plants are from Europe, Asia and North Africa. The name *hedera* comes from the Latin for ivy. They will climb up walls or similar structures or scramble along the ground, and are very vigorous. Species commonly grown are *Hedera canariensis* (syn. *H. algeriensis*, Canary Island ivy, North African ivy), *H. colchica* (Colchis ivy, Persian ivy), *H. helix* (English ivy) and *H. hibernica* (syn. *H. helix* subsp. *hibernica*, Atlantic ivy). They can become nuisances as groundcovers, or overtaking trees, if left to climb, so ideally need to be contained.

These plants are frost hardy, preferring shade or semi-shade.

Hedera canariensis

Pruning

If the ivy is trained as a groundcover, use hedge clippers to keep the growth low and compact, and to prevent it from spreading where you don't want it. For example, if it starts to grow up a tree, clip it back to ground level before it gets established in the tree.

If trained up a wall, clip back the growth in late spring to near the base. It will regenerate, even with a hard prune. Don't grow ivy up wooden structures such as the side of a house, as the roots will damage the woodwork. Regular pruning helps retain the juvenile foliage and stops the plant from flowering.

Propagation

From layers or stem cuttings.

Heliotropium arborescens
(syn. *H. peruvianum*)
Cherry pie, heliotrope

FAMILY: BORAGINACEAE

hardiness rating: 10–11

This evergreen, fragrant shrub comes from the mountains of Peru. The name *heliotropium* means turn to the sun, in reference to the flowers turning to the sun, while *arborescens* means tree-like. This shrub grows to about 2ft. 6 in. (75 cm) in height, and has fragrant, purple flowers from spring to fall. It prefers a frost-free site, with a well-drained soil.

Heliotropium arborescens

Pruning

Cut the plant back in early spring by nearly one-half, using pruning shears. Cut to a suitable node to get an even shape. Regular pruning will help to keep the plant bushy.

Propagation

From seed and stem cuttings.

Hibiscus syriacus 'Blue Bird'

Hibiscus syriacus
Blue hibiscus, Rose of Sharon

FAMILY: MALVACEAE

hardiness rating: 5–9

The word *hibiscus* comes from the Greek for marsh mallow. *Hibiscus syriacus* (Rose of Sharon) comes from Asia rather than Syria as the specific name *syriacus* would suggest. Cultivars include single, and a few double, flowers in shades of pink, white, blue and violet, often with dark, contrasting centers.

Like the tropical hibiscus, this plant needs full sun and good drainage but will tolerate colder conditions.

Pruning
Hibiscus can be kept in shape by trimming with hedge clippers or by cutting back to a suitable node with pruning shears. If plants have become spindly with age, cut back to 24 in. (60 cm) from the ground.

Propagation
From stem cuttings taken in spring or fall, or hardwood cuttings in winter.

Hoheria populnea

Hoheria populnea
Houhere, lace-bark

FAMILY: MALVACEAE

hardiness rating: 9–10

This evergreen tree from New Zealand grows to 20 ft. (6 m). The name *hoheria* comes from the Maori name for the tree. *Populnea* means poplar-like, in reference to the leaves. This plant produces a mass of white flowers over summer and fall, and often has a flaky, pale brown and white bark when mature, hence the common name lace-bark. There are variegated cultivars, such as *Hoheria populnea* 'Alba Variegata'.

Lace-barks are often used to provide a quick-growing shelter tree, as they are tolerant of most climatic conditions.

They can suffer from a dieback disease, and are susceptible to a mite that causes unsightly galls or lumpy growths on the stems.

Pruning Ψ
Hoherias are quick-growing, and if trained as a shelter tree may require pruning to keep them to a desired shape. Prune back to collars or lateral branches with a pruning saw to reduce the height or width of the tree. If they have become straggly, cut back harder, but always maintain some greenery. Take care with cutting branches with saws, as the lacy bark can easily tear. As always, undercut the branch first before making a final cut.

Propagation
From seed, or stem cuttings if a variegated cultivar.

Hydrangea
Hydrangea

FAMILY: HYDRANGEACEAE

hardiness rating: 4–9

This genus comprises mostly deciduous shrubs and climbers from East Asia and North and South America. The name *hydrangea* comes from the words *hydor*, water, and *aggos*, a vessel, in reference to the cup-shaped seed heads. They are grown mainly for their flowers, which make a spectacular display over summer. *Hydrangea macrophylla* (bigleaf hydrangea, florist's hydrangea) is the most commonly grown, the term *macrophylla* meaning large leaf. This species includes two types: the larger Moptop with its large blue or pink-red flowers, and the more delicate and smaller Lacecap type.

Hydrangea quercifolia

The color of the flowers is determined by the soil pH. Generally, acidic soils produce blue flowers while alkaline soils result in pink or red flowers. You can create acidic soils by adding aluminum sulfate, and alkaline soils by adding lime. Hydrangeas should be grown in good light, as they can become very leggy in the shade.

H. quercifolia (oakleaf hydrangea) is grown for its attractive foliage. The species name means oak-like leaves.

The climbing hydrangea, *H. petiolaris* (syn. *H. anomala* subsp. *petiolaris*), is ideal for shady areas where it can adhere to walls by its roots.

Like other plants, hydrangeas have flower buds that are fatter than the leaf buds. The stems of hydrangeas growing in the shade will be far more elongated, with most of the flower buds at the top. Those growing in the sun have flower buds throughout the plant. Cutting back hydrangeas hard, especially those growing in the shade, will result in a poor flowering.

Pruning

Often gardeners just cut back their hydrangeas in winter to a desired height, but this can result in a poor bloom the following summer. *H. macrophylla* can be pruned in winter once the flowers have finished and lost their color. If your hydrangeas have weak or non-productive shoots, remove all thin, poor growth to the base, using pruning shears. Leave about 6–12 of the main strong stems only, making sure that the plant has a balanced shape.

These stems will flower next year, so cut back about one-third to a node with two opposite buds if in the shade and to half-height if in the sun. The shaded plant is pruned lightly because most of the flower buds are at the top and heavier pruning would remove too many buds. If hydrangeas are growing well, all that may be needed is to remove dead flowerstalks back to the nearest pair of buds. Climbing hydrangeas can be trimmed back after flowering. As with other climbers that cling to walls, trimming back will ensure they don't get too heavy and come away.

Propagation

From semi-ripe stem cuttings taken in early summer and potted up as soon as rooted.

Hypericum calycinum

Hypericum calycinum
Aaron's beard, creeping St. John's wort, Rose of Sharon

FAMILY: HYPERICACEAE
hardiness rating: 5–9

This evergreen shrub comes from Southern Europe. The name *hypericum* comes from the Greek *hyper*, above, and *eikon*, picture or image, in reference to the resemblance of a figure of the upper parts of the flower. The plant has golden flowers, and is ideally grown as a groundcover on a bank. It can be grown in sun or semi-shade in a free-draining soil.

Hypericum is prone to the damage by thrips, which can be recognized by the silvering of the leaves.

Pruning

These plants can be cut back with hedge clippers almost to ground level every two or three years, and they usually regenerate well.

Propagation

From runners, divisions and seed.

Idesia polycarpa

Idesia polycarpa
Wonder tree

FAMILY: FLACOURTIACEAE
hardiness rating: 6–9

There is only one species of *Idesia*, and it is from Asia. The species name *polycarpa*, many fruit, refers to the prolific red berries. To get these berries you need both male and female plants. Both flower, but only the female plants carry the berries.

The wonder tree makes a stunning specimen, with clusters of brilliant berries hanging down in winter. It can reach 40 ft. (12 m) and has wide-spreading branches. *Idesia* tolerates frosts, making it ideal for inland areas, but prefers shelter from strong winds and adequate moisture over summer.

Pruning Ψ

As with all larger specimen trees, allow adequate room for growth. If more light is required underneath, the tree can be crown-raised. Cut back branches to a collar, undercutting the branch first to avoid tearing.

Propagation

They are best propagated by grafting so that you get the desired male and female plant or selected cultivar. They can be propagated from the seed but their sex will be unknown.

Ilex
Holly

FAMILY: AQUIFOLIACEAE
hardiness rating: 5–9

There are many deciduous and evergreen trees and shrubs of this genus found throughout the world. Berries of the more common *Ilex aquifolium* (English holly) are often used for Christmas decorations.

While English holly can grow to about 40 ft. (12 m), it is usually smaller because of its slow growth. As well as attractive red berries, it has glossy leaves which are spiny when young, and smooth at maturity. There are a number of cultivated hollies with variegated leaves. Like *Idesia* (wonder tree), you need male and female trees to get a good crop of berries. *I. crenata* (Japanese holly) is slightly hardier than I. aquifolium, and also has many useful cultivars. , some, such as 'Beehive', are useful as hedging plants.

Hollies are adaptable to different conditions, making them very hardy. They can be used as specimen trees or as hedges.

Pruning Ψ
These trees need little pruning if grown as specimens. Remove any straggly growth, using pruning shears, to keep them shapely. If grown as a hedge, trim each year in spring with hedge clippers, taking care to avoid the spines.

Propagation
Easily propagated from seed.

Ilex aquifolium

Jacaranda mimosifolia (syn. J. acutifolia, J. ovalifolia, J. ovatifolia)
Jacaranda
FAMILY: BIGNONIACEAE
hardiness rating: 9–11

This fast-growing deciduous tree from Brazil and Argentina can reach 50 ft. (15 m). The name *mimosifolia* refers to the mimosa-like leaves. The jacaranda has spectacular mauve-blue flowers, and makes an ideal specimen tree.

The jacaranda needs a warm, sunny climate where temperatures don't fall below 25°F (–4°C), shelter from strong winds and a free-draining soil that holds moisture.

Jacaranda mimosifolia

Pruning Ψ
Plants need to be staked when young. Pruning involves crown-raising to obtain a clean trunk. Remove lower branches back to the collar, using a pruning saw.

Propagation
From seed.

Jasminum
Jasmine, jessamine
FAMILY: OLEACEAE
hardiness rating: 6–11

Climbing jasmines, mostly from China, are vigorous plants. The popular *Jasminum polyanthum* is vigorous to the point of being invasive in gardens. Other species, such as *J. azoricum* (syn. *J. fluminense*), are less vigorous.

Jasmines are renowned for their scent and are ideally used where their roots can be restrained. They need training, so tie the tendrils to the structure

Jasminum polyanthum

they are growing on. Some make excellent groundcovers. They prefer full sun, and are moderately frost hardy.

Pruning

Pruning involves cutting back growth after flowering to keep the shape of the climber and to keep it compact. Cut back to a node, using pruning shears, or trim to shape with hedge clippers.

Propagation

While jasmine can spread rapidly, it takes time to grow from semi-ripe stem cuttings taken in fall. Runners can be cut up, and root very easily.

Juglans nigra

Juglans
Walnut

FAMILY: JUGLANDACEAE

hardiness rating: 3–9

These deciduous trees are from Southern Europe, the Middle East, Asia, North America and northern South America. They have attractive leaves, and some have edible nuts. *Juglans nigra* (black walnut) can grow to 100 ft. (30 m), while *J. regia* (English walnut) can reach 60 ft. (18 m).

The trees do best in full sun, and while generally frost hardy, young plants and spring growth are prone to frost damage. Plant in a free-draining soil with adequate moisture over summer.

Pruning Ψ

J. nigra can be crown-raised to give a clear trunk up to 15 ft. (4.5 m). Avoid pruning all walnuts in late winter or early spring, as they are prone to sap bleed at this time. *J. nigra* keeps a leader well, unlike *J. regia*, which may lose its leader due to frost damage. If this occurs, train a replacement to take over, and remove any competing leaders.

Propagation

From seed that has been stratified; cultivars are grafted.

Juniperus chinensis

Juniperus (syn. *Sabina*)
Juniper

FAMILY: CUPRESSACEAE

hardiness rating: 2–9

Widely distributed throughout the Northern Hemisphere, these evergreen conifers include trees, shrubs and groundcovers. The name *juniperus* is Latin for juniper.

They tolerate harsh conditions, including dry and coastal areas. They do, however, need good light to grow.

There is a huge range of species and cultivars. *Juniperus horizontalis* (creeping juniper) and its cultivars are groundcovers, as the species name suggests. *J. chinensis* (Chinese juniper) and its cultivars include shrubs and groundcovers.

Pruning

Little pruning is needed as the shrubby plants hold their shape well. The groundcover junipers can be easily controlled by pruning them back, with pruning shears, to the nearest node with a healthy shoot. As with other conifers, you cannot prune back junipers into older wood without causing dieback. Pruning needs to be targeted to retain foliage. Dieback can also be caused by insufficient light, especially at the base.

Propagation

From stem cuttings taken at any time of the year; they are slow to root.

Kalmia
Kalmia

FAMILY: ERICACEAE
hardiness rating: 2–8

These evergreen shrubs are from Northern United States and Cuba and are noted for their beautiful flowers. They are named after Peter Kalm, an 18th-century Swedish botanist.

Kalmia angustifolia (lambkill, sheep laurel, wicky) grows to 24 in. (60 cm), while *K. latifolia* (calico bush, mountain laurel) grows to 6–8 ft. (1.8–2.4 m).

Both shrubs prefer similar conditions to the related rhododendrons; that is, a cool, semi-shady position, such as beneath deciduous trees or on the cool side of a wall. They tolerate low temperatures, and prefer an acidic soil high in organic matter. Peat is an ideal mulch, which helps to reduce the need for cultivation or weeding, as these plants resent surface disturbance due to their mass of fine surface feeder roots. Kalmia are easily transplanted. As with all transplanting, particular care must be taken to avoid roots drying out in the process.

Kalmia latifolia 'Elf'

Pruning

Little pruning is required other than removal of the 3 Ds or criss-crossing branches with either pruning shears or a pruning saw. Remove the spent flowers with your forefinger and thumb, as you do for rhododendrons.

Propagation

K. angustifolia can be propagated from suckers, and *K. latifolia* from stem cuttings.

Kerria japonica

FAMILY: ROSACEAE
hardiness rating: 4–9

This deciduous shrub is from China originally, but long cultivated in Japan. It is the only species in the genus. The plant is named after William Kerr, an 18th-century gardener from Kew Gardens. The species name *japonica* means it is from Japan. It is notable for its intense yellow flowers in spring. Cultivars include *Kerria japonica* 'Pleniflora' with double flowers and *K.*

Kerria japonica 'Pleniflora'

japonica 'Variegata' with variegated gray-green leaves. They prefer good light but not hot sun, adequate moisture during summer, and are cold hardy to –68°F (–20°C).

Pruning
Because kerrias have a dense suckering habit, you can thin out the older stems by cutting them back to ground with a pruning saw. They flower on growth from the previous season, so you only need to remove stems older than two years, or ones that have finished flowering.

Propagation
From stem cuttings or from suckers arising from the base of the shrub.

Kniphofia
Red-hot poker, torch flower, torch lily

FAMILY: LILIACEAE
hardiness rating: 5–9

These mostly evergreen herbaceous perennials are from Southern Africa. They have showy pink, red, yellow and orange flowers in either winter or summer. *Kniphofia* x *praecox* is common in the wild, growing to 5 ft. (1.5 m), while *K. uvaria* grows to 4 ft. (1.2 m). There are a number of cultivars, each with different colored flowers.

Frost-hardy, they tolerate hot, dry conditions, including coastal areas.

Pruning
In late fall remove the dead flowers and leaves. Cut back the old flower stalks and leaves to the base using pruning shears.

Propagation
From seed or by division.

Kniphofia uvaria

Kolkwitzia amabilis
Beautybush

FAMILY: CAPRIFOLIACEAE
hardiness rating: 5–9

This deciduous shrub from China is the only species in the genus. It is named after Richard Kolkwitz, a botany professor from Berlin. The specific name *amabilis* means lovely, in reference to the pink flowers in spring, which are followed by pinky-brown fruits. The shrub is cold hardy to –68°F (–20°C), although late frosts may burn new growth. It prefers full sun and a free-draining soil with adequate moisture during drier periods.

Pruning
Beautybush needs little pruning, although older plants can have old wood cut back to a collar or a healthy node near the base with a pruning saw. Light thinning of stems that have flowered the year before will help to display the fruit, but avoid heavy pruning as this can remove next year's flowering wood.

Kolkwitzia amabilis

Propagation

From stem cuttings in summer or winter.

Kunzea

FAMILY: MYRTACEAE

hardiness rating: 8–11

These evergreen shrubs and small trees from Australia and New Zealand are named after Gustav Kunze, a 19th-century botanist. *Kunzea baxteri* has red bottlebrush-like flowers and grows to 6 ft. (1.8 m). *K. ericoides* (kanuka) has white flowers and can grow to 50 ft. (15 m). *K. parvifolia* has deep mauve flowers, and grows to 5 ft. (1.5 m). Kunzeas need a free-draining soil and full sun. They do not easily transplant when mature.

Kunzea parvifolia

Pruning

Like the related manukas, kunzeas can be pruned after flowering. Using either pruning shears or hedge clippers, cut back past the flowers. This will maintain bushiness and promote further blooms.

Propagation

From seed or stem cuttings.

Laburnum

FAMILY: FABACEAE

Golden chain tree, golden rain, laburnum

hardiness rating: 5–8

This genus consists of species from Europe and Western Asia. They are ideal as lawn specimens, with their drooping, yellow, pea-shaped flowers. *Laburnum anagyroides* (syn. *L. vulgare*, common laburnum) grows to 23 ft. (7 m), *L. alpinum* (Scotch laburnum) grows to 20 ft. (6 m), while *L.* x *watereri* is a hybrid of the two species. The cultivar *L.* x *watereri* 'Vossii' is a smaller tree that has very few or no seed pods. Laburnums are frost-hardy, and prefer full sun and a free-draining soil.

Laburnum anagyroides

Pruning

Train and, if necessary, temporarily stake the trees from an early age. Remove lower branches up to 6 ft. (1.8 m) back to the collar, using a pruning saw. Cut criss-crossing branches back to a collar. Laburnums are used to create archways, using two rows of trees with their branches tied down over a trellis, pergola or tunnel.

Propagation

From seed that has been soaked, or by grafting cultivars or hybrids.

Lagerstroemia indica

FAMILY: LYTHRACEAE

Crape myrtle, crepe myrtle

hardiness rating: 7–9

Lagerstroemia indica is the main species grown of these deciduous and evergreen trees and shrubs. *Lagerstroemia* is named after Magnus von

91

Lagerstroem, an 18th-century merchant, while *indica* means Indian, although the plants originate from China and Korea. *L. indica* grows up to 25 ft. (7.6 m). It is notable for its crape paper-like flowers borne during summer and fall, and its attractive bark. There are many cultivars and hybrids with flowers in white, lavender, pink or crimson.

The trees need full sun and warmth, with a free-draining, slightly acidic soil.

Pruning

Remove spent flower heads by cutting back to a node past the flowers using pruning shears, and remove all deadwood. You can train shrubs as single trunks with a rounded head, or multi-stemmed bushes. If you want a single trunk, remove all lateral branches back to the collar to the desired height. To get a rounded head, keep cutting back shoots to a node to create a sphere. To maintain a multi-stemmed bush, cut back all the stems to a node once the desired height is reached.

Propagation

From seed or stem cuttings.

Lagerstroemia indica

Larix
Larch

FAMILY: Pinaceae

hardiness rating: 1–8

This genus includes 12 species of deciduous conifers distributed through the Northern Hemisphere. *Larix decidua* (syn. *L. europaea*, European larch) can grow to 100 ft. (30 m), and *L. kaempferi* (syn. *L. leptolepis*, Japanese larch) grows to the same height. Young plants are grafted to get a weeping effect.

Larches are commonly used in forestry plantings, but if space allows, one would make an ideal specimen tree with its brilliant fall foliage. *Pseudolarix* is a close relative of larch, and is also an excellent specimen tree. All tolerate cold climates and prefer free-draining soils.

Pruning Ψ

Little pruning is required if the tree is given adequate space to grow. If it gets insufficient light, lower branches tend to die off, and are self-pruning.

Propagation

From seed that has been stratified or by grafting if hybrids or cultivars.

Larix decidua

Laurus nobilis
Bay laurel, sweet bay

FAMILY: Lauraceae

hardiness rating: 8–10

This evergreen tree with aromatic leaves is from Southern Europe. The name *laurus* comes from Latin, while *nobilis* means notable or famous. The young laurel shoots were used in ancient Greece as the crown of laurel for victors. The tree's fruiting sprays provided funeral wreaths for poets and priests. The leaves have always been used for culinary purposes, and the oil from the berries for perfume.

While it can grow to 40 ft. (12 m), bay laurel is often trained into formal shapes and is popular for topiary work. It can be grown in containers or as a hedge.

The tree is frost hardy to 23°F (−5°C), will tolerate coastal winds, and grows in sun or semi-shade.

Laurus nobilis

Pruning Ψ

If a standardized form is desired, remove the lower branches of a sapling until you get to the required height, and then clip back the stems to a node to get the desired shape. If used as a screen, trim regularly with hedge clippers to maintain bushiness. Remember to leave the base of the hedge wider then the top so that sun and light can maintain healthy bottom growth. Once the desired height is reached the hedge can be clipped on the top and sides twice a year.

Propagation

From seed or stem cuttings.

Lavandula
Lavender

FAMILY: LAMIACEAE
hardiness rating: 5–10

These colorful shrubs and perennials are mostly from the warm Mediterranean area. The name lavender comes from the Latin *lavo*, to bathe, and refers to the traditional use of lavender oils when bathing.

Lavenders are very popular because of their fragrance and long flowering period. They are commonly used as hedges as their neat gray foliage trims easily. They are also ideal among perennials, where their gray foliage acts as a nice background.

Common species and their cultivars are *Lavandula angustifolia* (English lavender, lavender), *L. dentata* (fringed lavender) and *L. stoechas* (French lavender).

As they come from a hot climate, lavenders prefer full sun and good drainage.

Lavandula stoechas subsp.
penduncularis

Pruning

Prune after flowering to maintain a compact shape and good future flowering. Cut back to the nearest node with pruning shears or use hedge clippers. If you leave lavenders unpruned for too long, they can get woody at the base.

Cutting back older plants too hard can cause dieback, so trim back at least once a year.

Propagation

From softwood or semi-ripe stem cuttings taken from spring to fall. Use a free-draining mix, such as pumice, as the cuttings do not like wet feet.

Lavatera thuringiaca

Lavatera
Mallow

FAMILY: MALVACEAE

hardiness rating: 7–10

This genus is related to the mallows and hollyhock, and is found in temperate climates like the Mediterranean. It includes annuals, biennials and herbaceous and woody perennials, although the latter are short-lived.

All are grown for their flowers, most successfully if given a free-draining soil and full sun.

Pruning

After flowering, cut back past the flowers to the nearest node, using pruning shears. This will promote bushiness and further flowering.

Propagation

From seed, or from stem cuttings for the perennial types.

Leonotis leonurus

Leonotis leonurus
Lion's ear, lion's tail

FAMILY: LAMIACEAE

hardiness rating: 10–11

This evergreen, shrubby perennial comes from South Africa. The name *leonotis* comes from the Greek *leon*, a lion, and *ous*, an ear, from the resemblance of the flower to a lion's ear. The specific name *leonurus* comes from the Greek *leon*, lion, and *ouros*, a tail, referring to the resemblance of the whole flower to a lion's tail.

This plant grows to 6 ft. (1.8 m), bearing orange flowers in summer and fall. Like other members of the Lamiaceae or mint family, the leaves are aromatic. The plant tolerates dry conditions and light coastal winds.

Pruning

The long stems of orange blooms can be picked as cut flowers, trimmed back to a node with pruning shears. After flowering, cut back one-half to nodes with pruning shears. This will kept the plant compact and improve flowering. If left, the plant becomes tall and straggly.

Propagation

From rooted shoots that have formed at the base, or from cuttings taken over the warmer months.

Leptospermum scoparium
Manuka, New Zealand tea tree

FAMILY: Myrtaceae
hardiness rating: 8–10

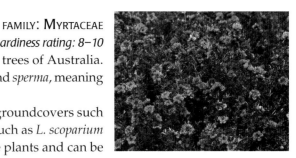

Manuka is a New Zealand native tree related to the tea trees of Australia. The generic name comes from the Greek *leptos*, narrow, and *sperma*, meaning seed, referring to the narrow seeds.

There are many cultivars of manuka, ranging from groundcovers such as *Leptospermum scoparium* 'Red Falls', to taller shrubs such as *L. scoparium* 'Wiri Joan' and *L. s.* 'Crimson Glory'. They are versatile plants and can be used for mass planting on banks or in mixed plantings. Their attractive flowers appear at different times of the year, depending on the cultivar.

Leptospermum scoparium 'Crimson Glory'

Manuka grows in a wide range of conditions, including dry coastal places through to swampy areas.

Plants can suffer from a sooty mold that develops on honeydew produced by a scale insect. However, this mold can be controlled if necessary with a suitable insecticide.

Manuka are not easy to transplant as the fine roots are liable to be damaged in the process.

Pruning
The cultivars are the most commonly grown and, as with all tea trees, can be cut back after flowering, though they will not tolerate hard pruning into old wood. Therefore, cut them back each year with pruning shears, past the finished flowers, shaping the plant as needed.

Leaving shrub manuka unpruned can result in them becoming woody and flowering only at the tips.

Propagation
L. scoparium is easily propagated from seed, while the cultivars are grown from softwood and semi-ripe stem cuttings taken from spring to fall.

Leucadendron
Leucadendron

FAMILY: Proteaceae
hardiness rating: 8–10

These shrubs and trees come from South Africa, mostly the Cape area. The name comes from the Greek word *leucos* meaning white, and *dendron*, tree, in reference to the silvery leaves of *Leucadendron argenteum* (silver tree), one of the Cape's most beautiful species. Other popular leucadendrons include *L. tinctum* (tolbos) and *L. salignum*. Hybrids 'Safari Sunset' and 'Silvan Red' offer striking cut flowers, having been bred for that market.

Leucadendrons mostly have attractive small to medium flowers surrounded by colorful bracts. As members of the protea family they prefer acidic soils free of phosphates. They are ideal for coastal areas, where their silvery, hairy or leathery leaves are especially suited to tolerate full sun and coastal winds. They have a fine mass of roots and resent being shifted once they are over 3 ft. (1 m).

Leucadendron 'Safari Sunset'

95

Pruning

As with member of the protea family, use pruning shears to cut back after flowering to a node just past the spent flowers. If picking the flowers, then the pruning can be done at the same time.

Leucadendrons will not regenerate if you cut back into old wood. Regular light pruning will result in a more compact bush with better flowering.

Propagation

From seed or softwood or semi-ripe stem cuttings. The seed should be soaked first and cuttings are best taken from summer to fall.

Leucothoe fontanesiana 'Rainbow'

Leucothoe fontanesiana (syn. *L. catesbaei*)
Drooping leucothoe, fetterbush

FAMILY: ERICACEAE

hardiness rating: 5–8

This evergreen shrub is native to Southeastern United States. The genus is named after the same Leucothoe of Greek mythology, while the species name honors Rene Desfontaines, an 18th-century botanical author.

The shrub's leaves turn bronzy purple in fall, and in late spring white flowers, looking like lily-of-the-valley, appear. Plants require similar conditions to the related pieris and rhododendrons; that is, part shade, and slightly acidic soils that are high in organic matter.

Pruning

Flowers are borne on new growth, so hard pruning will encourage flowering. Old flowering stems can be cut back to a collar. Pruning can take place from fall to early spring. If growth becomes rank and untidy, you can cut back all stems to ground level with a good likelihood of new regenerative growth occurring.

Propagation

From seed or cuttings.

Liquidambar styraciflua

Liquidambar styraciflua
Liquidambar, Sweetgum

FAMILY: HAMAMELIDACEAE

hardiness rating: 7–9

Liquidambar styraciflua is probably the most widely grown of these deciduous trees from the Northern Hemisphere. The name is derived from *liquidis* (liquid) and *ambar* (amber) referring to the resin called storax. Sweetgums are renowned for their bright fall foliage and make attractive street trees. Broadly conical, they can grow to about 80 ft. (24 m). There are a number of cultivars, such as *L. styraciflua* 'Burgundy' and *L. styraciflua* 'Worplesdon'.

Sweetgums prefer a moist, slightly acidic soil and show off their leaves best when sheltered from strong winds. They are difficult to transplant once over 6 ft. (1.8 m).

Pruning Ψ

Pruning should be confined to creating a good shape with a single main stem, if grown as a specimen. They can be crown-raised as the tree grows taller. Many of these trees fail due to having included bark (inwardly formed bark at the junction of branches or co-dominant stems).

Propagation

From seed or by grafting. They can also be raised from root cuttings.

Liriodendron
Tulip tree

FAMILY: MAGNOLIACEAE

hardiness rating: 5–9

This genus includes two species from China, Indochina and North America. The generic name is from the Greek *leirion*, a lily, and *dendron*, a tree. They are an ancient relative of magnolias, and are renowned for their unusual foliage and tulip-like flowers.

 Liriodendron tulipifera (tulip tree, yellow poplar) is native to East North America, includes a number of cultivars, and can grow to 100 ft. (30 m). The leaves turn yellow in the fall, and the flowers bloom in summer. The specific name *tulipifera* means tulip-bearing, referring to the flowers. *L. chinense* (Chinese tulip tree) comes from China as the specific name suggests, and can grow to 80 ft. (25 m).

 Tulip trees need a slightly acidic, free-draining soil and full sun, sheltered from the prevailing wind. They are difficult to transplant.

Liriodendron tulipifera
'Aureomarginata'

Pruning Ψ

L. chinense makes a good leader without training, but *L. tulipifera* needs to have any rival leaders removed. The tree should be crown-raised by removing branches back to collars up to a trunk height of 15–20 ft. (4.5–6 m).

 Many of these trees fail due to having included bark (inwardly formed bark at the junction of branches or co-dominant stems).

Propagation

From stratified seed or by grafting for the selected cultivars.

Lithodora diffusa

FAMILY: BORAGINACEAE

hardiness rating: 7–10

This evergreen, low-growing plant comes from Southern Europe. Many gardeners still know it as *Lithospermum*. The name *lithodora* comes from the Greek *lithos*, a stone, and *doron*, a gift. The plant is grown for its intense blue flowers, and is used in rock gardens or to cover banks or walls. There are a number of cultivars, such as *Lithodora diffusa* 'Grace Ward' and *L. d.* 'Heavenly Blue'.

 This plant needs full sun and a free-draining soil that is slightly acidic. It can tolerate temperatures down to 5°F (–15°C).

Lithodora diffusa

Pruning

Prune after flowering to keep the plant dense and promote further flowering. They can be trimmed lightly with hedge clippers past the spent flowers.

Propagation

From stem cuttings taken from late spring to fall.

Lonicera caprifolium

Lonicera
Honeysuckle

FAMILY: CAPRIFOLIACEAE

hardiness rating: 5–9

This genus includes about 180 species of shrubs and climbers found throughout the Northern Hemisphere. It is named after Adam Lonitzer, a 16th-century German botanist.

- *Lonicera* x *americana* is a deciduous climber growing up to 23 ft. (7 m) with fragrant, yellow flowers tinged with purple.
- *L. caprifolium* (Italian woodbine) is a deciduous climber that can reach 20 ft. (6 m) and has fragrant white to yellow pink-tinged flowers in summer followed by orange-red berries.
- *L. japonica* (Japanese honeysuckle) is an evergreen climber growing to 23 ft. (7 m) with very fragrant flowers, which age from white to yellow in the cultivar 'Halliana'.
- *L. nitida* (boxleaf honeysuckle) is a small-leaved shrub from China that is normally used as a hedge.
- *L. periclymenum* (common honeysuckle, woodbine) is a deciduous climber growing to 20 ft. (6 m) with yellow-white, very fragrant flowers.
- *L. sempervirens* (coral honeysuckle, trumpet honeysuckle) is an evergreen climber growing to 12 ft. (3.6 m) with orange-scarlet flowers.
- *L* x *tellmanniana* is a deciduous climber growing to 15 ft. (4.5 m) with unscented coppery orange flowers.
- *L. tragophylla* is a deciduous climber growing to 15 ft. (4.5 m) with large, long-tubed orange-yellow flowers.

Honeysuckles are very hardy, can grow in most soils and in full or partial sun. In warmer climates the climbers can be very vigorous.

Pruning

L. nitida needs to be regularly trimmed with hedge clippers if trained as a hedge. Trim the sides and tops twice a year during the growing season.

The climbers need to be trained up a structure, and their tendrils attached. They can get very overgrown, so you should thin out about a quarter of the older shoots back to the base of the plant in spring.

Propagation

From stem cuttings or layers.

Loropetalum chinense
Fringe flower

FAMILY: HAMAMELIDACEAE
hardiness rating: 8–9

This evergreen shrub is the main one grown of the two species found in the Himalayas, China and Japan. The name *loropetalum* comes from *loros*, a strap, and *petalon*, a petal, referring to the long, narrow petals, which are very similar to closely related hamamelis. It has these picturesque white, scented flowers in spring, and graceful, spreading branches.

It will grow in sun or semi-shade, in a slightly acidic soil that is free-draining and rich in organic matter.

Loropetalum chinense

Pruning
With its horizontal growth, this shrub can be trained as an espalier. It can be pruned after flowering to contain its size, but make sure you retain the attractive spreading branches.

Propagation
By stem cuttings in summer or fall.

Luculia

FAMILY: RUBIACEAE
hardiness rating: 9–11

These evergreen shrubs come from East Asia. *Luculia* is derived from *lukuli swa*, which is the Nepalese name for this plant.

Luculia grandifolia has white flowers and beautiful leaves. It flowers in late summer, through fall and in winter. *L. gratissima* bears pink flowers in late fall and winter. Both are fragrant. They are semi-evergreen, which means they drop a proportion of their leaves unless the site is very warm. They need a sunny area, free of frost, with free-draining soil.

Luculia gratissima 'Early Dawn'

Pruning
With pruning shears, cut back to a node after flowering to prevent them becoming too leggy. This will encourage new growth and better flowering. Older plants can have their older stems cut back to the base to encourage new growth.

Luculias do not like being transplanted when they are over 5 ft. (1.5 m).

Propagation
From seed or semi-ripe stem cuttings taken in fall.

Magnolia
Magnolia

FAMILY: MAGNOLIACEAE
hardiness rating: 3–9

This genus contains a huge range of trees and shrubs, most of which are deciduous. When choosing, check their eventual height and spread as they vary considerably.

• *Magnolia stellata* (star magnolia) is deciduous, reaching 6 ft. (1.8 m).

Magnolia denudata

- *M. denudata* (lily tree, Yulan magnolia) is also deciduous, reaching 30 ft. (9 m).
- *M. campbellii* is a deciduous tree growing to 80 ft. (25 m), with a crown spreading up to 40 ft. (12 m) wide.
- *M. grandiflora* (bull bay, southern magnolia) is evergreen and grows up to 80 ft. (25 m).

Magnolias make magnificent specimen trees or features in the garden and their flowers are spectacular and often scented. They prefer full sun and shelter from strong winds. Mulching around the roots helps to maintain a cool root zone, as enjoyed in their natural environment. Magnolias have fleshy roots and resent root disturbance of any kind. They should not be transplanted once established.

Pruning Ψ

These plants need little pruning if they are given the space to grow. Remove the 3 Ds to maintain good health and to shape the plant, especially if it is unbalanced. Likewise, you can raise the crown if light or access is a problem. The evergreen *M. grandiflora* can be crown-reduced by one-third without ill effect, as long as all cuts are to collars or lateral branches. Avoid pruning the deciduous trees in spring as the sap may bleed.

Propagation

From seed that has been cooled in the fridge for 12–16 weeks. Stem cuttings can be taken from spring to fall or they can be propagated by grafting.

Mahonia lomariifolia

Mahonia
FAMILY: Berberidaceae
Holly grape, mahonia
hardiness rating: 6–10

Hardy evergreen shrubs in this genus are from Northwestern United States and the Orient. They are named after Bernard McMahon, a 19th-century American horticulturist. They are related to *Berberis* with their colorful fragrant flowers, grape-like berries and dramatic foliage. *M. bealei* (syn. *M. japonica* 'Bealei', leatherleaf mahonia) grows to 7 ft. (2.1 m), *M. japonica* to 6 ft. (1.8 m), and *M. lomariifolia* to 10–15 ft. (3–4.5 m).

Mahonias grow best in semi-shade, protected from strong winds in a free-draining, slightly acidic soil.

They can be affected by leaf spot fungi and caterpillars.

Pruning

Little pruning is required, but if plants get old and leggy they can be cut back to ground level with a pruning saw to promote new healthy growth. As they have prickly leaves, you may need gloves.

Propagation

From seed or stem cuttings.

Malus
Apple, crabapple

FAMILY: ROSACEAE

hardiness rating: 3–8

These deciduous trees and shrubs from Northern Europe are grown for their flowers or fruit. The name *Malus* comes from the Latin word for apple.

Apart from the fruiting cultivars, there are many ornamental hybrids and cultivars. The crabapples are so named for the sharp taste of the fruit.

Ornamental *Malus* make good specimen or street trees. They need full sun and shelter from strong winds.

Apples are prone to a number of diseases, such as black spot, silverleaf and fireblight. Using a copper spray over winter is recommended.

Malus floribunda

Pruning

There are various ways of training apples, as discussed in the section on fruit trees in the Introduction. They form good espaliers, which has the advantage of easy picking, and horizontal branching that encourages fruiting. For domestic use they can be trained as a central leader or open vase shape.

Many of the problems I have come across when pruning apples arose because they have been overpruned. Remember that they flower on wood that is two or more years old. Pruning established plants too hard creates a mass of new growth that won't flower for two years.

Minimal pruning is usually all that is needed, but young plants need to be trained to form a good strong framework to carry fruit later.

The trees you purchase should have a number of branches arising from the main stem. During the first year select the strongest four branches. Prune these branches back by two-thirds after fruiting. Cut back with strong pruning shears or loppers. Cut to a node with the bud facing outwards with a sloping cut. For the next two years, cut these branches back by one-half in the same way. Remove any weak branches to their collars.

After this the framework should be established. Further pruning should be confined to thinning out the fruiting spurs as they get older and to shaping the tree as needed. Espaliered apples need to be trained from an early age. You can create as many tiers as you wish.

Ornamental apples need little pruning other than the removal of 3 Ds or lower branches.

Propagation

From budding a cultivar on to a rootstock. While you can grow apples from seed, you will get an inferior seedling compared with a budded specimen.

Maytenus boaria

Maytenus boaria (syn. *M. chilensis*)
Mayten

FAMILY: CELASTRACEAE
hardiness rating: 9–10

This graceful evergreen tree is from Chile. *Maytenus* comes from *maiten*, a Chilean name for this tree. The species name *boaria* means of cattle, as they forage on the leaves. It has a habit like a weeping willow, but without the invasive roots, growing up to 25 ft. (7.6 m) in height and width. The tree prefers full sun and free-draining soils, and will tolerate temperatures down to 14°F (–10°C). Mayten trees are drought tolerant, but will maintain more growth if watered regularly during dry periods.

Pruning Ψ
Make sure the tree has adequate room to grow. Stake the young tree securely in exposed locations. Unless you want a multiple-trunked specimen, remove the competing leaders back to the collar with a pruning saw.

Propagation
From stem cuttings taken during the growing season.

Melia azerdarach

Melia azerdarach
**Bead-tree, chinaberry, Persian lilac,
Pride of India**

FAMILY: MELIACEAE
hardiness rating: 8–11

This deciduous tree is native to India and China. *Melia* comes from the Greek for ash, while *azerdarach* is from the Persian word for noble tree. It is a rapid-growing tree, reaching 30 ft. (9 m). Its attractive foliage, flowers and fruit makes it an ideal landscape specimen. The bead-tree is wind and drought hardy, but needs protection from frost when young.

Pruning Ψ
The natural growth habit of a bead-tree is a single stem with a spreading crown. It is best to have a clear trunk up to 10 ft. (3 m), so maintain a good single trunk by removing any competing growth when the tree is young. Cut back any lateral branches to a collar with a pruning saw.

Propagation
From seed, or by root cuttings or stem cuttings for selected forms.

Metasequoia glyptostroboides
Dawn redwood

FAMILY: TAXODIACEAE
hardiness rating: 5–10

This deciduous conifer is a native of Western China, where it was found only in fossil records until a live specimen was discovered in 1941. *Metasequoia* comes for the Greek *meta*, different, and *sequioa*, a genus to which it is related. *Glyptostroboides* comes from *glyptos*, carved, and *strobus*, cone, in reference to the cone formation.

The dawn redwood can grow to 65 ft. (20 m), and is used as a specimen or forestry tree. While it can be trained as a hedge, it is not suitable as it puts on too much top growth.

This tree is ideally grown near rivers, as it does best in moist soil conditions. It is cold hardy but prefers hot summers.

Pruning Ψ
If trained as a tree, remove competing leaders. As it is a vigorous grower, it will quickly make new growth.

Propagation
From stratified seed or stem cuttings.

Metasequoia glyptostroboides

Michelia
Michelia

FAMILY: MAGNOLIACEAE

hardiness rating: 9–11

These evergreen shrubs and trees come from Southeast Asia, India and Sri Lanka. They are named after Pietro Antonio Micheli, an 18th-century Florentine botanist. There are a number of species grown for their attractive foliage and highly fragrant flowers. *Michelia doltsopa* from the Himalayas can grow to 30 ft. (9 m), and has scented white flowers. *M. doltsopa* 'Silver Cloud' offers gardeners a prolific flower production. *M. figo* (syn. *M. fuscata*, banana shrub, port wine magnolia), from Western China, grows to 10 ft. (3 m), and has scented cream flowers.

Michelias prefer a free-draining soil high in organic matter that is neutral to acidic. Grow them in sun or shade in areas free from all but light frosts.

They transplant more readily than the closely related magnolias.

Michelia doltsopa

Pruning Ψ
These shrubs and trees need little pruning other than the removal of the 3 Ds, and can be crown-raised or lowered as required.

Propagation
From stem cuttings.

Morus
Mulberry

FAMILY: MORACEAE

hardiness rating: 5–9

These deciduous trees and shrubs are mostly from Eastern Asia. *Morus nigra* (black mulberry) is grown for its fruit, *M. rubra* (red mulberry) from Southeast Canada and Eastern United States also has edible fruit but is mainly grown as an ornamental, and can reach 70 ft. (21 m). *M. alba* (syn. *M. bombycis*, white mulberry, silkworm mulberry) from China and Japan, can grow to 40 ft. (12 m). Its leaves were used as a food source for silk worms.

Morus nigra

The fruit of *Morus nigra*

Mulberries have invasive root systems, so take care not to plant them near drains. They grow well in full sun, a sheltered location and fertile, free-draining soils.

Pruning Ψ

Little pruning is needed other than the removal of the 3 Ds.

Propagation

From stem cuttings or by grafting.

Myrtus communis var. *italica*

Myrtus communis
Common myrtle, true myrtle

FAMILY: MYRTACEAE

hardiness rating: 8–9

This Mediterranean, evergreen shrub grows to 10 ft. (3 m). The name *myrtus* comes from the Greek and Latin for myrtle. Myrtles can be used as hedges or grown in containers. *Myrtus communis* and a number of its cultivars are grown for their perfumed white flowers and distinctive foliage.

They prefer sun or light shade and free-draining soils with adequate moisture.

Pruning

Regular trimming will keep the plants compact. If grown as a hedge, trim the tops and sides to maintain bushiness with hedge clippers once a year.

Propagation

From seed or, in the case of varieties, from cuttings.

Nandina domestica

Nandina domestica
Heavenly bamboo, sacred bamboo

FAMILY: BERBERIDACEAE

hardiness rating: 6–9

The only species of this genus is native to the region from India to Japan. *Nandina* comes from the Japanese word *nandin*, while *domestica* means used as a house plant. It is valued for its beautiful foliage, flowers and berries. There are a number of cultivars, such as the low-growing *Nandina domestica* 'Nana' (syn. 'Pygmaea'), or *N. domestica* 'Richmond', which grows to 6 ft. (1.8 m).

This plant is cold hardy to 5°F (–15°C), and grows in sun or partial shade, but has more intense leaf color in full sun. If the soil is too alkaline, add iron sulfate to correct the chlorosis or yellowing of the leaves.

Pruning

Old stems that have become straggly can be cut to ground level in spring using a pruning saw, especially on taller plants like *N. domestica*. The new growth that will come away will be helped with the addition of a general-purpose fertilizer.

Propagation
From tip stem cuttings.

Nothofagus
Southern beech

FAMILY: FAGACEAE

hardiness rating: 7–10

This genus consists of 25 or more species found throughout the Southern Hemisphere. Mostly fast-growing, large trees, those native to New Zealand can be considered the southern counterpart of the European beech. The name *Nothofagus* comes from the Greek *nothos*, false, and *fagus*, beech. The beeches in the Northern Hemisphere are members of the *Fagus* genus.

These trees can reach great heights. For example, *Nothofagus fusca* (red beech) can reach 100 ft. (30 m). *N. menziesii* (silver beech) grows to 80 ft. (25 m). They are usually too large for suburban gardens unless the property backs on to forest or open space. *N. solandri* (black beech) grows to a more modest 50 ft. (15 m).

Beeches make ideal specimen trees for parks and if trained from an early age they also make good hedges. These trees grow in full sun or semi-shade, but prefer shelter. They do not survive prolonged drought or waterlogging. Like most trees, they cannot tolerate soil being heaped around the base of the trunk. This can cause collar rot, which results from the persistent dampness and lack of air around the tree's base and can eventually kill it.

Nothofagus solandri var. *cliffortioides*

Pruning Ψ

If grown as a specimen tree in an ideal location beeches should need little pruning other than removal of the 3 Ds. Try to keep one central leader. If two leaders develop, remove the weaker one when it is young.

Specimens that are not in ideal conditions, or grown in exposed locations, can form a lot of deadwood.

If trained as a hedge, space plants about 3–5 ft. (1–1.5 m) apart. Trim once a year during active growth, along the sides and lightly at the top, until the desired height is reached.

Propagation
From fresh seed.

Nyssa
Tupelo

FAMILY: NYSSACEAE

hardiness rating: 5–9

These deciduous trees are native to Eastern North America and Southeast Asia. The name *nyssa* means a water nymph, referring to the swampy habitat of some species. *Nyssa sinensis* (Chinese tupelo) has brilliant red and yellow color, and grows to 30–50 ft. (9–15 m). *N. sylvatica* (black gum, sour gum, tupelo) has bright red and vivid orange leaves in fall and can grow to 70 ft. (21 m).

Nyssa sylvatica

Plant tupelo near lakes or ponds in a moist soil that is neutral or slightly acidic. They can grow in sun or partial shade.

Pruning Ψ
Remove the 3 Ds and any criss-crossing branches. When young, train a good leader, removing any weaker ones, as well as lower branches up to 6 ft. (1.8 m) to get a clear trunk.

Propagation
From stratified seed, stem cuttings or grafting.

Olea europaea

Olea europaea
Olive

FAMILY: Oleaceae

hardiness rating: 8–10

This fruiting cultivated evergreen tree from the Mediterranean is a relative of jasmine and forsythia.

Olives require well-drained alkaline soils, full sun and a frost-free area. Young trees in exposed locations can be staked until the roots have developed and the tree is firm in the ground. If you are growing the trees for fruit, cool temperatures over winter will help boost the tree into vigorous growth for spring flowering and prolific fruit set. When the fruit has set, additional watering may help with a good fruit size and high oil content, but the main requirement is a long and hot summer.

Pruning
Remove the 3 Ds and by thinning retain sufficient light in the center of the tree. Prune to restrict height annually, after fruit is harvested in fall. Deadwood can be removed at any time. Winter damage can be cut back to a suitable collar or lateral branch in spring.

Propagation
From seed or cuttings.

Olearia paniculata

Olearia
Daisy bush, olearia

FAMILY: Asteraceae

hardiness rating: 7–11

These evergreen shrubs are from New Zealand and Australia. The name *olearia* comes from *olea*, olive, in reference to the similarity of the leaves of some species to those of olives.

Olearias are mostly grown for their foliage, although some species such as *Olearia cheesmanii* (syn. *O. rani*) have spectacular flowers. They can also be trained as excellent hedges, especially *O. traversii* and *O. paniculata*.

Olearias are very tolerant plants, growing well in coastal conditions and dry soils.

Pruning

If trained as a hedge, plant 3 ft. (1 m) apart and prune each year during the growing season. Trim along the sides and lightly on the top until you reach the desired height.

O. traversii becomes woody and open if left unpruned, so trim back with hedge clippers or pruning shears each year. Cut back the lanky growth to a node so that the tree looks balanced.

Other shrubby specimens need little pruning apart from removal of the 3 Ds. Olearias can become infested with borer, which may leave hollow stems. While it doesn't usually affect their growth it can lead to structural branch or stem failure, particularly in exposed locations.

Propagation

From stem cuttings or seed.

Osmanthus (syn. x *Osmarea, Siphonosmanthus*)   FAMILY: OLEACEAE
Osmanthus

hardiness rating: 6–10

These evergreen trees and shrubs are native to Southern United States, the Middle East, China and Japan. The name comes from the Greek *osme*, fragrance, and *anthos*, flower, referring to the richly fragrant flowers. The leaves are serrated, and look like holly.

Osmanthus x *burkwoodii* (syn. x *Osmarea* x *burkwoodii*) and *O. delavayi* (syn. *Siphonosmanthus delavayi*) grow to 6 ft. (1.8 m), while *O. fragrans* (fragrant olive, sweet olive) grows to 10 ft. (3 m). *O. heterophyllus* (false holly) has a height and spread of 15 ft. (4.5 m).

Osmanthus x burkwoodii

Grow these plants in sun or partial shade in a free-draining soil that is slightly acidic.

Pruning

To maintain a bushy habit, cut the longer stems back to a node closer to the main growth, using pruning shears. This should be done after flowering in fall. As all osmanthus are slow growing, pruning can be done as needed.

Propagation

From stem cuttings.

Paeonia
Peony

FAMILY: PAEONIACEAE

hardiness rating: 3–8

These deciduous herbaceous perennials and shrubs are native to Eurasia, with two species from North America. The name *paeonia* goes back to classical Greek and arises for the species supposed medicinal properties. *Paeonia suffruticosa* (moutan, mudan, tree peony) is from China, and grows to 7 ft. (2.1 m). Like the other two tree peonies, *P. delavayi*, which grows to 6 ft. (1.8 m), and *P. lutea*, which grows to 8 ft. (2.4 m), these plants are soft-

Paeonia lactiflora

107

wooded shrubs. Most of the cultivars of the herbaceous peonies come from *P. lactiflora* (syn. *P. albiflora*, *P. japonica*), which originates in China.

Peonies need a cold winter, but the new growth and flowers can be damaged by late frosts. They all need a deep soil with plenty of organic matter, good light and a sheltered position.

Pruning
Prune in early spring. Cut back the old flower stalks to the nearest bud, using pruning shears. Remove any deadwood at the same time.

Propagation
From seed that has been stratified, or by division for herbaceous cultivars, and grafting for tree peonies.

Parthenocissus tricuspidata

Parthenocissus
FAMILY: Vitaceae
Boston ivy, Japanese ivy, Virginia creeper
hardiness rating: 3–10

These deciduous climbing plants come from North America and Asia. The genus is named from the Greek *parthenos*, virgin, and *kissos*, ivy. One of their main features is brilliant fall foliage. They are generally frost hardy and prefer well-drained soils. Protect from hot, drying winds.

Popular species include *Parthenocissus henryana*, *P. quinquefolia* (Virginia creeper) and *P. tricuspidata* (Boston ivy) — all have good fall color.

Pruning
These climbers cling neatly to flat structures and need little pruning other than removal of growth away from windows, gutters and trees. They are ideally trained to grow up stone or brick buildings, especially as the suction cups at the end of each tendril can damage wooden houses. They should be pruned each year in fall–winter. Use pruning shears to cut back unwanted growth to a node.

Propagation
From semi-ripe stem cuttings taken in summer–fall, or hardwood cuttings in winter.

Paulownia tomentosa

Paulownia tomentosa (syn. *P. imperialis*)
FAMILY: Bignoniaceae
Empress tree, foxglove tree, princess tree, royal paulownia
hardiness rating: 5–8

This deciduous tree from Central and Western China is named after Anna Paulowna, daughter of Paul I, Tsar of Russia. Some paulownia can be used for timber and paper, but this species makes a fine ornamental shade tree with its large heart-shaped leaves and beautiful lilac flowers. It grows very quickly, soon reaching 50 ft. (15 m).

P. tomentosa prefers full sun, and protection from strong winds. It is frost hardy to 5°F (–15°C) when established, but needs protection when young. In cold climates, the flower buds can be damaged in winter, and plants can be damaged or die after very heavy "wet" frosts.

Pruning Ψ

As these trees grow very quickly, pruning will result in strong new growth. They can be coppiced or pollarded to encourage even bigger leaves. If you wish to reduce the height of the tree, and get more leafy growth and flowers lower down, you can reduce the crown height by cutting to suitable lower lateral branches. The wood is very light and easy to handle.

Propagation

From seed, stem or root cuttings.

Penstemon
Penstemon

FAMILY: SCROPHULARIACEAE
hardiness rating: 3–10

These evergreen or semi-evergreen herbaceous perennials or shrubs are nearly all from the Western United States. The name comes from the Greek *pente*, or five, and *stemon*, stamens, in reference to the fifth stamen being sterile.

There are numerous species and cultivars grown for ornamental use. *Penstemon heterophyllus* (foothill penstemon) grows to 18 in. (45 cm) and has blue flowers. *P. pinifolius* is an evergreen plant reaching 12 in. (30 cm), with scarlet flowers.

Penstemons need sun or part shade, and a well-drained soil.

Penstemon heterophyllus

Pruning

Deadhead the spent blooms over the summer to prolong flowering. Foliage damaged in winter should be allowed to remain as protection until frosts are past, then in spring cut back to healthy growth with pruning shears.

Propagation

From seed or by stem cuttings for the cultivars.

Perovskia atriplicifolia
Russian sage

FAMILY: LAMIACEAE
hardiness rating: 6–9

This low-growing, deciduous shrub comes from Afghanistan. It bears panicles of fragrant, purple-blue flowers in summer and fall. These are well complemented by the soft gray-green aromatic foliage.

Russian sage needs a well-drained soil and full sun. It is very frost hardy.

Perovskia atriplicifolia

Pruning

Prune back hard in early spring. Cut back shoots to one or two buds from the base with pruning shears.

Propagation

From seed or stem cuttings taken in spring and summer.

Persea americana

Persea americana
Avocado

FAMILY: LAURACEAE

hardiness rating: 10–11

This evergreen tree is grown for its fruit, and is native to South America. It can grow to 60 ft. (18 m). While the tree is self-fertile, at least two are needed for reliable fruiting. The avocado is frost tender, need full sun, shelter from strong winds, and a soil that is free-draining yet provides adequate moisture when the tree is fruiting.

Pruning

Little pruning is required other than the removal of the 3 Ds. The crown can be raised by removing the lower branches.

Propagation

The fruiting varieties are grafted on to seedling rootstock.

Philadelphus coronarius

Philadelphus coronarius
Mock orange

FAMILY: HYDRANGEACEAE

hardiness rating: 5–8

This deciduous shrub originates from Southern Europe and the Caucusus. The name *philadelphus* comes from the Greek for brotherly love.

Mock oranges are noted for their white or cream, fragrant flowers in summer, and are ideal companions in borders of perennials or bulbs. There are other species in cultivation, but the main one is *Philadelphus coronarius* and its cultivars, or the hybrids such as *P.* 'Virginal'.

These plants require full sun, good drainage and tolerate frost. They prefer alkaline soil, so lime can be added.

Pruning

P. coronarius will often flower prolifically year after year with no pruning. The flower buds arise from the previous year's growth. Older, woody plants can be pruned nearly to the ground to rejuvenate them, but they won't produce flowers until the following spring.

If your shrub is flowering well, and its size and shape are suitable, then pruning may be unnecessary. If not, cut back the older growth to ground level and the newer growth to a node where a strong, healthy shoot is arising. Use pruning shears or loppers for thicker growth.

Propagation
From hardwood stem cuttings taken in winter.

Phoenix canariensis
FAMILY: Arecaceae

Canary Island date palm, phoenix palm
hardiness rating: 9–11

This large palm from the Canary Islands can grow to 40 ft. (12 m). *Phoenix* is the Greek name for the date palm.

With their wide heads and thick trunks, these palms form an impressive specimen on a lawn or along an avenue, but because of the height and spread, they are not recommended for urban gardens. These palms are surprisingly hardy but need frost protection and adequate water when young. They also require full sun and good drainage.

Phoenix canariensis

Pruning Ψ
As with most palms, pruning is restricted to removing the lower fronds. Because the fronds are thick, use a pruning saw to cut them back as close as possible to the trunk. Be extremely careful of the spines at the base of the fronds; they are needle sharp and can inflict painful wounds requiring hospital treatment. The fronds can be left alone as old ones eventually drop off, but this can look unsightly and could be dangerous if people are walking beneath the palm when an old frond is shed.

Removing a phoenix palm is an expensive operation as the dense nature of the trunk makes cutting with chainsaws difficult. Make sure you plant this palm where it has adequate room to grow.

Propagation
Like other palms, *P. canariensis* is propagated from seeds, but these are slow to germinate.

Phormium
FAMILY: Agavaceae

Mountain flax, New Zealand flax
hardiness rating: 7–10

These evergreen, herbaceous perennials are from New Zealand and Norfolk Island. The name comes from *phormion*, from the Greek for mat, referring to the strong fibers produced from the leaves. They are grown for their attractive sword-like leaves and tall flower spikes. *Phormium cookianum* (syn. *P. colensoi*, mountain flax) is found only in coastal or alpine areas, while *P. tenax* (New Zealand flax) is found in swampy areas. They are both very tolerant of most conditions, but *P. tenax* can grow in permanently wet soils. There are many colorful cultivars that are used ornamentally.

Flaxes can get a leaf spot disease, which can be treated with fungicides, and caterpillar damage is often a problem.

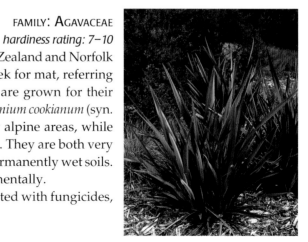

Phormium tenax 'Tom Thumb'

Pruning
If planted in the correct location, these plants need little pruning. If planted

near pathways, they will need regular cutting back. If you need to reduce their size, cut back the outer leaves to the base with a sharp knife or a pair of pruning shears. They can be divided to keep them in good shape.

Propagation

From seed, or by division in the case of the cultivars. Cut the leaves so the divided plant has a triangular shape.

Photinia serrulata

Photinia (syn. *Heteromeles, Stranvaesia*)   FAMILY: ROSACEAE
Photinia   *hardiness rating: 6–10*

These deciduous and evergreen trees and shrubs are mostly native to Japan and China. The name *photinia* comes from the Greek word *photos*, light, in reference to the shining leaves.

Possibly the most popular of these shrubs is *Photinia* x *fraseri* 'Red Robin' (red tip), which was developed in New Zealand. Its bright red foliage makes an eye-catching hedge or stunning feature plant. While most of the photinias grown are shrubs up to 10 ft. (3 m), *P. serrulata* (syn. *P. serratifolia*) is a tree, which can grow to 30 ft. (9 m).

These plants all tolerate wind but need good drainage and full sun. Some photinias are prone to fireblight, a bacterial disease that also affects other members of the Rosaceae family such as apples. This disease causes blackening of the bark or branch dieback, and is best treated by removing infected branches or whole plants if necessary.

Pruning Ψ

If growing as a hedge, plant 3 ft. (1 m) apart. Regular trimming is needed during the growing season; use hedge clippers to cut the side and top growth. Due to its rapid growth, you may need to trim the plant twice a year. They will respond with a mass of new red growth.

Older specimens that have become too woody at the base can be cut almost to ground level with a pruning saw and have a good chance of regrowth providing the plant is otherwise healthy.

Trees like *P. serrulata* can have the 3 Ds removed and be crown-raised if space and light are required.

Propagation

From softwood and semi-ripe stem cuttings taken from summer to fall.

Picea   FAMILY: PINACEAE
Spruce   *hardiness rating: 2–9*

These evergreen conifers are from the Northern Hemisphere. The name comes from the Latin *picea*, from *piceus*, or pitch, referring to the resins in the tree.

Spruces are tolerant of heavy frosts, but prefer a sheltered location with ample water during establishment. They differ from *Abies* by the small, rough, peg-like projections left on the stems when the leaves are removed, and mature cones hang down rather than face upwards.

- *Picea abies* (Norway spruce) grows from 60 to 100 ft. (18–30 m).
- *P. brachytyla* (sargent spruce) is a more tender species than most of the spruces at recommended hardiness zones 8–9. It grows to 80 ft. (25 m).
- *P. omorika* (Serbian spruce) reaches 50 ft. (15 m).
- *P. pungens* (Colorado spruce) also grows to 50 ft. (15 m) and the species has many cultivars, such as *P. pungens* 'Koster', which has silvery blue leaves.

Spruces are prone to spruce aphid, especially *P. abies* and *P. pungens*.

Picea brachytyla

Pruning Ψ

These trees need little pruning other than the removal of deadwood, and establishing a good straight main stem.

If the central leader gets damaged, prune back to another suitable lateral branch. Using a pruning saw, cut above the new branch at an angle.

Propagation

From stratified seed, or by grafting selected forms.

Pieris
Fetterbush, lily-of-the-valley bush, pearl flower, red-leaf

FAMILY: ERICACEAE
hardiness rating: 3–9

These evergreen shrubs are native to East Asia, the Himalayas, Eastern North America and the West Indies. They are named after Pieria, a place in Greece which was supposed to have been the home of a muse in Greek mythology.

Pieris floribunda (fetterbush, mountain pieris) grows to 6 ft. (2 m) and has dark foliage. The white flowers appear in early spring. *P. formosa* has a popular garden cultivar *P. formosa* var. *forrestii* 'Wakehurst'. It has brilliant red new foliage in spring followed by white flowers, and grows to 10 ft. (3 m). *P. japonica* (lily-of-the-valley bush) is a compact shrub growing to around 12 ft. (4 m). It flowers very early in the season, the white blooms appearing in late winter and spring. This species has many very attractive cultivars, including 'Christmas Cheer', which has pink flowers with dark pink tips.

Pieris japonica 'Valley Valentine'

Pieris do best in similar conditions to rhododendrons, to which they are related. Grow them in semi-shade in an acidic soil that is rich in organic matter. Like rhododendrons they are prone to thrip infestation. Due to their dense, fibrous roots, they are easily transplanted.

Pruning

Little pruning is required as they naturally hold their shape well. If you wish to reduce the size of the shrub, prune back to suitable lateral branches with a pruning saw.

Propagation

From seed, or stem cuttings taken from spring to fall if the plant is a hybrid or cultivar.

Pinus nigra

Pinus
Pine

FAMILY: PINACEAE

hardiness rating: 3–10

These are evergreen conifers from the Northern Hemisphere. The name *pinus* is thought to come from the Latin word for pitch, in reference to the resinous sap.

There are many species of pine, most of them large trees requiring ample room to grow.

- *P. mugo* (mogo pine, mountain pine) is the dwarf of the pines, growing 12–14 ft. (3–4 m).
- *P. nigra* (Austrian pine, European black pine) can reach 100 ft. (30 m).
- *P. patula* (Mexican yellow pine) has a graceful habit and grows up to 50 ft. (15 m).
- *P. pinea* (stone pine, umbrella pine) grows to 30 ft. (10 m)
- *Pinus radiata* (syn. *P. insignis*, Monterey pine, radiata pine) can grow to 120 ft. (36 m).
- *P. wallichiana* (syn. *P. chylla*, *P. excelsa*, *P. griffithii*, Bhutan pine, blue pine, Himalayan pine) grows to 60 ft. (18 m).

Pines are very tolerant of extreme climates (from inland, frosty areas to coastal areas) but they do need good drainage. Most pines do not grow well in soils that are alkaline.

Pruning Ψ

Pruning forestry trees is a separate subject altogether, where the aim is to get straight trunks with minimal branching. Radiata pine and other pines are also used as a shelter hedge for farming and horticulture, and training and pruning needs to start at an early age.

For trees used ornamentally, the most important thing is to choose the right plant for the location so that its natural shape can grow unimpeded.

Cut back any dieback to a collar using a pruning saw. Crown-raising can be used to improve light and access for larger trees. Aim to preserve the main leader of larger trees, so remove any weaker leaders before they get too large.

Watch out for the sticky resin as it will stain your skin and clothes!

Propagation
From seed or by tissue culture for high-quality forestry trees.

Pittosporum
Pittosporum

FAMILY: PITTOSPORACEAE
hardiness rating: 8–10

This genus consists of some 200 species of mostly evergreen trees and shrubs from Asia, Africa, Australisia and the Pacific islands. The name *pittosporum* comes from the Greek *pitta*, pitch, and *spora*, seed, in reference to the sticky, black seed of some species.

Pittosporum tenuifolium cultivars in the foreground

All the species of pittosporum native to New Zealand are very popular ornamentals. They are planted for a wide range of uses, from specimen trees to hedging. Some make excellent coastal shelter, such as *Pittosporum crassifolium* (karo). The many cultivars of *P. tenuifolium* (kohuhu) are very diverse in color and form. *P. eugenioides* (lemonwood, tarata) is one of the larger pittosporums, growing to 15 ft. (4.5 m), sometimes more.

Pittosporums are hardy plants but prefer full sun, adequate drainage and moisture over summer. They do not transplant readily as they do not form a good, fibrous rootball and their woody roots tear easily.

Pruning Ψ
If growing as a hedge, space plants about 3 ft. (1 m) apart. They need trimming twice a year while they are actively growing. Trim the sides with hedge clippers and lightly trim the top until the desired height is reached. Specimen trees such as *P. eugenioides* should have the 3 Ds removed. Allow them to grow to their natural height, only reducing this if absolutely necessary by pruning back to the nearest lateral branch with pruning shears or loppers.

Propagation
From fresh seed. The sticky seed can be mixed with pumice or sand to make it easier to handle. Cultivars are propagated from softwood or semi-ripe cuttings taken from spring to fall.

Platanus
Plane, sycamore

FAMILY: PLATANACEAE
hardiness rating: 5–9

These deciduous trees are from North America, Southwest Europe, Southwest Asia and Indochina. They are named after the Greek word for plane, *platanos*, which is derived from *platys*, meaning broad or flat, referring to the leaves. *Platanus* x *acerifolia* (syn. *P.* x *hispanica*, London plane) grows to 80–120 ft. (25–36 m), as does *P. occidentalis* (buttonwood, sycamore). *P. orientalis* (Oriental sycamore) grows to 80–100 ft. (25–30 m).

The above species are all ideal as trees for city areas, as they tolerate poor soil, a good proportion of hard surfacing over their root zone, and air pollution.

Platanus x *acerifolia*

115

Pruning Ψ

As the trunk and bark are features, a clean stem up to 15 ft. (4.5 m) is ideal. Nursery plants are usually grown with clean stems of 8 ft. (2.4 m).

It is essential that all these trees have adequate room to grow. Planes have been traditionally pollarded in many cities. However, this practice can have a long-term weakening effect on the trees, and today you are just as likely to see them grown out into their normal height.

Propagation

From stratified seed or by stem cuttings taken in winter.

Plumbago auriculata

Plumbago auriculata (syn. *P. capensis*)   FAMILY: PLUMBAGINACEAE
Cape leadwort   *hardiness rating: 9–10*

This evergreen shrub comes from South Africa. The name *plumbago* is derived from the Latin *plumbum*, lead, in reference to its supposed ability to remedy lead poisoning.

Plumbago auriculata has phlox-like blue flowers over spring and summer. The blooms of it cultivar 'Royal Cape' are a more intense blue and 'Alba' has white flowers.

Because of their semi-climbing nature, these plants are ideal for growing up walls or fences. They require full sun, good drainage and shelter.

Pruning

If training up a structure, keep the plants shaped to control growth and encourage flowering. After flowering, prune back to a node past the flowers with pruning shears. Cut back to encourage the form you want to achieve.

Propagation

From softwood or semi-ripe stem cuttings taken from spring to fall.

Podocarpus   FAMILY: PODOCARPACEAE
hardiness rating: 7–10

Evergreen trees and shrubs in this genus come from all over the world. The name *podocarpus* comes from *podos*, a foot, and *karpos*, fruit, in reference to the fleshy foot-like aril that supports the seeds.

The plants are very adaptable in their uses. *Podocarpus nivalis* (alpine totara) from New Zealand is a groundcover, ideal for rockeries, and *P. totara* (totara), also from New Zealand, can be used as a specimen tree or a hedge. As a tree it can grow up to 100 ft. (30 m). The cultivar 'Aurea' has a attractive gold leaf color.

All the many species of podocarps prefer full sun, good drainage, and adequate moisture. They ideally should be sited with other plants for protection.

Podocarpus totara 'Aurea'

Pruning Ψ

If training totara as a hedge, plant 3 ft. (1 m) apart. They are slow-growing and require only minimal pruning with pruning shears or hedge clippers to keep the sides trimmed and the top even.

As a tree, totara will need little pruning if it has adequate room and light. It can develop a lot of deadwood lower down and removing this will improve the appearance of the tree. Crown-raising can highlight the attractive trunk with its peeling bark.

Propagation

From seed or from semi-ripe stem cuttings for *P. totara* 'Aureus', the golden yellow cultivar of totara.

Populus
Aspen, cottonwood, poplar

FAMILY: SALICACEAE

hardiness rating: 3–9

Populus balsamifera

These deciduous trees are from Northern Europe. The name *populus* comes from the Latin word for poplar.

- *Populus balsamifera* (balsam polar, tacamahac) is a fast-growing tree with attractive yellow leaves in the fall. It can reach 100 ft. (30 m), as can another species from North America, *P. trichocarpa* (black cottonwood, Western balsam poplar).
- *P. nigra* 'Italica' (Lombardy poplar), perhaps the most widely known poplar, grows in a narrow column to 100 ft. (30 m) very quickly and is not a long-lived tree. It has leaves which turn an intense yellow in fall.
- *P. yunnanensis* (Chinese poplar) forms a spreading tree up to 60 ft. (18 m), but care is needed as the buds drop resin that can be damaging to houses and cars.

Because of their large size, poplars must have space to grow. They make excellent wind breaks or avenue trees lining a long driveway. Because of their invasive roots they need to be kept away from paths, lawns or old drains.

They are very hardy, tolerating damp conditions as well as drought once they are established. Lombardy poplar is attacked by rust fungi, but the Chinese poplar is resistant to rust.

Pruning Ψ

Lombardy poplars form upright growth with one single leader. This means they seldom need pruning for shape if they have adequate space to grow. The poplars with spreading growth habits can be crown-raised or lowered. Pruning back to a collar can result in a mass of epicormic shoots but this spindly growth can be cut back each year with a saw.

Poplars are easily transplanted, but larger specimens should have their top growth shortened back to a suitable bud before they are moved.

Propagation

From hardwood stem cuttings taken in winter. Like willows, they can be started with large pieces of stem, up to 6 ft. (1.8 m) long buried about 12 in. (30 cm) into the ground, from where they will root freely.

Protea neriifolia

Protea
Protea

FAMILY: PROTEACEAE
hardiness rating: 9–10

These beautiful evergreen shrubs come from South Africa, mostly from the Cape region. The name comes from *Proteus*, the Greek mythological figure who changed shape at will, in reference to the great diversity of form of the species.

Proteas' large, colorful flowers bloom over winter and spring. There are many species and cultivars, with *Protea neriifolia* and its many cultivars being popular. *P. cynaroides* (king protea) has very large blooms.

As they come from South Africa these shrubs demand hot, dry conditions. Like all members of this family, they prefer acidic soils and cannot tolerate phosphates in the soil. The best location for them is a sunny bank near the coast, where good drainage and adequate air movement are ideal. Proteas have surface roots that are very prone to damage so you must avoid digging around them. They will not transplant.

Pruning

The best time to prune is when you pick the blooms. Cut back to a suitable node using pruning shears. If the blooms are left, wait until they are finished and then cut back to a node as described. This will keep the plant compact, encourage new growth and remove what would be unsightly dead flower heads.

Like other members of this family, such as leucadendrons, proteas will become woody at the base if left unpruned. You can't prune back into old wood as the plant will suffer dieback. Older plants in this condition are probably best removed. Regular pruning will keep the plant compact and free-flowering.

Propagation

From seed, but the germination is erratic. It helps to soak the seed in hot water before sowing. They can also be propagated from stem cuttings taken in summer and fall.

Prunus cerasifera 'Pissardii'

Prunus (syn. *Amygdalus*)

FAMILY: ROSACEAE
hardiness rating: 6–8

This genus includes a huge range of deciduous trees from the Northern Hemisphere, South America and Southeast Asia. The name *prunus* is Latin for plum tree and this genus includes a range of edible stone fruits (cherries, plums, apricots, peaches, nectarines and almonds). There are also many very beautiful ornamental species, most notable the Japanese flowering cherries.

Whether ornamental or fruiting, these shrubs and trees all need full sun, protection from late or early frosts and shelter from strong winds. Moisture is important over dry periods especially while becoming established.

Because of the importance of some of the species in this genus, they have been given separate entries below.

Prunus
Plum

FAMILY: ROSACEAE

hardiness rating: 5–9

Some *Prunus* species that are commonly known as plums produce edible fruits, whereas others are very popular as ornamental plants, for example *P. cerasifera* (cherry plum, myrobalan). The ornamentals especially are notable for their colorful leaves and flowers.

P. x domestica (common plum, European plum) has numerous cultivars and is grown mainly for its fruit. It quickly reaches 30 ft. (10 m), or more, and its white flowers are borne in spring.

P. salicina (Japanese plum) produces a less juicy fruit and these are considered best used in cooking, or drying for prunes.

Prunus x domestica 'Fortune'

Pruning
Japanese plums (*P. salicina*) bear fruit on the previous year's lateral branches and spurs. Remove old unproductive spurs and thin the laterals in the same way as nectarines and peaches.

European plums (*P. x domestica*) produce fruit on spurs that develop on wood that is in its second year. Therefore they need less pruning than the Japanese plums, being more like apples. The fruiting spurs remain productive for many years. Pruning involves removing deadwood and thinning out old spurs.

Both types of plum shouldn't be pruned in winter or early spring to avoid sap bleeding or the risk of fungal diseases, especially silverleaf.

Propagation
From budding or grafting on to a rootstock.

Prunus armeniaca
Apricot

FAMILY: ROSACEAE

hardiness rating: 5–9

There are both ornamental and fruiting apricots. The ornamental ones, such as *Prunus mume* (Japanese apricot), are noted for their flowers, which are ideal for indoors.

Whether ornamental or fruiting, they need full sun, protection from late or early frosts and shelter from strong winds. All too often you see a magnificent display of flowers in spring and then watch it disappear in the spring gales.

Prunus armeniaca

119

Moisture is important over dry periods, especially when the tree is becoming established.

Pruning

- *Ornamental:* The aim of pruning ornamental apricots should be to get a well-formed tree. Removing the lower branches will provide better access under the tree. Always remove branches to the collar. The best time to prune these plants is after flowering. Don't prune in winter or early spring because the sap can flow from the wounds and the risk of fungal diseases is greater. If removing flowers for indoors, cut the stem back to a node.
- *Fruiting:* These plants bear fruit on spurs that develop on wood at least two years old. They become less vigorous with time. Some varieties flower on one-year-old wood. Pruning should aim to renew fruit spurs. Remove unfruitful branches back to the collar, and allow new lateral branches to replace this growth. Don't prune in winter or early spring.
- Cultivars that fruit on one-year-old wood should be pruned like peaches. (See next entry.)

Propagation

By budding or grafting on to suitable rootstocks.

Prunus persica 'Texstar'

Prunus persica
Flowering peach, nectarine, peach

FAMILY: Rosaceae
hardiness rating: 6–9

There are both ornamental and fruiting peaches. *Prunus persica* reaches 12 ft (3.6 m) or more, and has a profusion of pinkish-red flowers in early spring. *P. persica* var. *nectarina*, the nectarine, is almost identical in habit to the peach, but has different fruit.

Both ornamental and fruiting varieties need full sun, protection from late or early frosts and shelter from strong winds. Moisture is important over dry periods, especially when trees are first being established.

Peaches and nectarines can develop a fungal disease called leaf curl, which can disfigure the plant. Using a copper spray starting prior to bud burst will help to control it.

Pruning

- *Ornamental:* The aim of pruning ornamental peaches is to get a well-formed tree. Removing the lower branches will provide better access under the tree. Always remove branches to the collar. The best time to prune is after flowering. Don't prune in winter or early spring because the sap can flow from the wounds and the risk of fungal diseases is greater. If removing flowers for indoors, cut the stem back to a node.

- *Fruiting:* These trees bear fruit on shoots produced the previous summer. Hence, harder pruning is needed to encourage new lateral branches to form fruit. Using pruning shears, remove any laterals that have produced fruit back to the branch collar. In the same way, thin out the laterals that will fruit the following spring to prevent overcrowding. Don't prune in winter or early spring because the risk of fungal disease or sap bleeding is higher during these periods. Older plants can have their height reduced to encourage growth lower down.

Propagation
From budding or grafting on to a suitable rootstock.

Prunus serrulata
Japanese flowering cherry, oriental cherry

FAMILY: ROSACEAE

hardiness rating: 5–8

While there are both ornamental and fruiting cherries, the ornamental Japanese flowering cherries, such as those of the *Prunus*, Sato-zakura group, make beautiful specimen trees or focal points in the garden. There are countless upright and weeping cultivars, most developed in Japan. The species *P. serrulata* is a spreading tree, growing to 30 ft. (10 m).

P. x *subhirtella* (Higan cherry, rosebud cherry) is another graceful Japanese cherry and it enjoys a cooler climate. It also has many desirable cultivars, most of which produce a profusion of pink flowers in the spring.

Whether ornamental or fruiting, they need full sun, protection from frosts and shelter from strong winds. All too often a magnificent display of flowers in spring disappears in the spring gales. Moisture is important over dry periods, especially while getting established.

Prunus subhirtella var. 'Rosea'

Pruning
- *Ornamental:* The aim of pruning ornamental cherries is to get a well-formed tree. Removing the lower branches will provide better access. Remove branches to the collar. The best time to prune is after flowering. Do not prune in winter or early spring because the risk of fungal diseases and sap bleeding is greater. If removing flowers for indoors, cut the stem back to a node.
- *Fruiting:* Like the ornamental types, the fruiting plants should ideally be pruned in summer to reduce the likelihood of fungal diseases such as silverleaf infecting the plant. These plants bear fruit on long-lived spurs, which remain productive for 10 to 12 years. Little pruning is needed other than removal of the 3 Ds and shaping to the desired form. When they grow large, reduce the height to encourage growth lower down. Cut back to suitable lateral branches with loppers or pruning saw.

121

Propagation
From budding or grafting on to suitable rootstocks.

Pseudopanax 'Gold Splash'

Pseudopanax

FAMILY: ARALIACEAE
hardiness rating: 8–10

The New Zealand evergreen shrubs from this small genus of Southern Hemisphere plants include many with very unusual foliage. The name *pseudopanax* comes from the Greek *pseudo*, false, and *panax*, meaning not a true panax.

Pseudopanax crassifolius (lancewood) has distinctive juvenile and adult stages. As a juvenile it has long, narrow, sword-like leaves with a single stem, while the adult has a bushy head with shorter leaves. *P. ferox* (toothed lancewood) has similar leaves to lancewood, but the edges are more pronounced. *P. lessonii* (houpara) has many hybrids, popular examples being *P.* 'Purpureus' with purple foliage and *P.* 'Gold Splash' with yellow-splashed leaves.

Pseudopanax can tolerate cold as well as heat, but do need good drainage. They are ideal as container plants, background foliage plants or as a feature plant, especially the lancewood. These plants can be transplanted with care if not too large.

Pruning Ψ
The lancewood should not need pruning as its form is distinct and its growth controlled.

Other *Pseudopanax* can have the 3 Ds removed to maintain health and vigor. The crown can be reduced to keep them compact or it can be raised to improve light or access. To reduce the height, prune to the nearest healthy lateral branch with a pruning saw. If removing lower branches, cut back the branch to a collar using a pruning saw. The plants make rapid regrowth after pruning.

Propagation
From fresh seed, but the hybrid cultivars need to be propagated from semi-ripe stem cuttings taken in summer and fall.

Psidium guajava
Common guava, yellow guava

FAMILY: MYRTACEAE
hardiness rating: 10–12

These evergreen fruiting trees are natives of Central America. The name *psidium* comes from the Greek word for pomegranate. They grow to 30 ft. (9 m), and prefer a warm, frost-free area, fertile soil and protection from the wind.

Psidium guajava

Pruning

Fruit is borne on new growth arising from mature wood. A framework of four branches should be developed, and any unwanted growth thinned out. Remove any deadwood or spindly growth back to a collar using a pruning saw. Guavas also sucker, so remove any suckering growth with a pruning saw back to the base.

Propagation

From seed or by grafting.

Punica granatum
Pomegranate

FAMILY: PUNICACEAE
hardiness rating: 8–10

This is the cultivated species of the two deciduous shrubs or small trees which make up the genus. They are native to the East Mediterranean and Palestine. The name *punica* comes from *puniceus*, Latin for red, referring to the flower or fruit. *Granatum* means many seeds, referring to the abundant seeds in the red fruit. Grown since antiquity, the pomegranate prefers hot, dry conditions, and is ideal as a container plant. Cultivars include *Punica granatum* 'Pleniflora', with double orange-red flowers, and *P. granatum* 'Nana Plena', a low-growing form. 'Wonderful' is an example of a form selected for fruiting.

Pruning

Little pruning is required, but pomegranates can be kept to a desired size by using pruning shears to cut back to nodes in summer after they have flowered.

Punica granatum

Propagation

From seed, or stem cuttings for the cultivars.

Pyracantha
Firethorn

FAMILY: ROSACEAE
hardiness rating: 5–9

These evergreen shrubs are from Europe and Asia. The botanical name comes from *pyr*, fire, and *akanthos*, thorn, in reference to its common name. The shrubs produce colorful berries in fall and winter. *Pyracantha* 'Brilliant' bears scarlet berries and those of *P.* 'Shawnee' are orange.

Firethorns tolerate hot, dry conditions, making them ideal as a cover for a bank. They can also be trained as a hedge or up a wall. However, they are prone to the bacterial disease fireblight, which, as is the case with cotoneaster, is difficult to eradicate.

Pruning

The flowers and berries are produced from the previous year's growth. As the berries are the main feature, pruning should aim to encourage their

Pyracantha 'Brilliant'

display. After flowering, prune back any protruding growth to a node, using pruning shears, but avoid damaging or pruning any developing berries. When the berries are in color, you can remove any growth that hides them.

If training as a hedge, plant about 24 in. (60 cm) apart and trim once a year on the sides and top until the desired height is reached. If training the plant on a wall, select strong leaders, and remove any shoots that come out from the wall. Cut this growth back with pruning shears to the collar. Watch out for the prickly thorns.

Propagation
From seed or from stem cuttings taken any time.

Pyrus communis 'Durondeau'

Pyrus
Pear

FAMILY: ROSACEAE

hardiness rating: 4–9

Deciduous trees and shrubs in this genus come from the Northern Hemisphere. The name *pyrus* is Latin for pear. There are fruiting pears, mainly *Pyrus communis* (common pear) and Asian pears. *P. salicifolia* 'Pendula' (weeping silver pear, weeping willow-leaved pear) is an ornamental and makes an attractive focal point in the garden. Pears need full sun and good drainage.

Pruning
The ornamental weeping pear can be bought as a trained standard or a small tree. Pears should not need pruning apart from keeping the shape of the tree. Cut back any unwanted growth to a node or collar.

There are various ways of training fruiting pears as described in the section on fruit trees in the Introduction. They form good espaliers, which provide easy picking, and encourage fruiting. For domestic use they can be trained with a central leader or in an open vase shape.

A great many of the problems I have come across when pruning pears and apples have been due to overpruning. Remember that they both flower on wood that is two or more years old. If you prune established plants too hard you create a mass of new growth that won't flower for two years.

If anything, only minimal pruning is needed, other than training young plants to form a good strong framework to carry the fruit later.

The trees you purchase should have a number of branches arising from the main stem. During the first year select the strongest four branches. Prune these branches back by two-thirds after fruiting. Cut back, with either strong pruning shears or loppers, to a node with the bud facing outwards with a sloping cut. For the next two years cut these branches back by one-half in the same way. Remove any weak branches to their collars.

After this, the framework should be established and further pruning should be confined to thinning out the fruiting spurs as they get older. You can also shape the tree as needed.

Espaliered pears should be trained from an early age. You can create as many tiers as you wish. (See page 25 for training espaliers.)

Propagation
Fruiting and weeping pears are propagated by budding or grafting on to suitable rootstock.

Quercus
Oak

FAMILY: FAGACEAE

hardiness rating: 3–10

There are about 500 species of deciduous and evergreen trees in this genus with a very wide distribution. The name *quercus* is Latin for oak.

- *Quercus cerris* (Turkey oak) is a deciduous tree growing to 100 ft. (30 m).
- *Q. coccinea* (scarlet oak) is a deciduous tree with brilliant red leaves in fall, growing up to 70 ft. (21 m).
- *Q. ilex* (holly oak, holm oak) is an evergreen tree that reaches 80 ft. (25 m) that tolerates coastal conditions.
- *Q. palustris* (pin oak) is a deciduous tree growing to 60 ft. (18 m) with red leaf color in fall.
- *Q. petraea* (syn. *Q. sessiliflora*, durmast oak) is a deciduous tree growing to 100 ft. (30 m).
- *Q. robur* (syn. *Q. pedunculata*, English oak, pendunculate oak) is a fast-growing deciduous tree with a height and spread of up to 80 ft. (25 m). *Q. robur* 'Fastigiata' has a more narrow upright growth habit, ideal for smaller areas.
- *Q. rubra* (syn. *Q. borealis*, northern red oak) is a deciduous tree that reaches 80 ft. (25 m) with red leaves in fall.
- *Q. suber* (cork oak) grows to 60 ft. (18 m) and is the source of commercial cork.

Oaks need a soil that retains moisture and is slightly acidic.

Quercus palustris

Pruning Ψ
You need to develop a single leader, by removing any competing side branches back to their collars with a pruning saw. There can be a lot of variation among nursery-grown trees, with some readily forming multiple leaders. Try to select plants with a strong leader at the time of purchase. As the trees develop, you can raise the crown by removing lower branches up to 8–10 ft. (2.4–3 m) back to the collar. Removal of the 3 Ds should be done as needed, especially *Q. robur*, which can suffer crown dieback due to lack of light within the crown.

Propagation
From stratified seed.

Raphiolepis x *delacourii*
'Enchantress'

Raphiolepis (syn. *Rhaphiolepis*)
Indian hawthorn

FAMILY: Rosaceae
hardiness rating: 8–10

These evergreen shrubs come from Southeast Asia. The botanical name comes from the Greek *rhapis*, a needle, and *lepis*, a scale, referring to the bracts around the flower. The common name refers to the fact that true hawthorn is in the same family.

Among the more frequently grown garden varieties are *Raphiolepis* x *delacourii*, a hybrid growing to 6 ft. (1.8 m) and *R.* x *delacourii* 'Enchantress', growing to 3 ft. (1 m). Both these shrubs have pink flowers. *R. umbellata* (syn. *R. japonica*, *R. ovata*) grows to 10 ft. (3 m) and has white, scented flowers.

These shrubs are very tolerant of hot, dry conditions and are ideal for coastal gardens.

Pruning
These shrubs can be left unpruned as their natural growth habit is usually compact. Any branches that die back should be cut back to a collar with pruning shears. If a more open growth habit is required, thin out some of the weaker shoots by pruning back to a collar with pruning shears during the growing season. To achieve a more dense growth, cut back to a node past the flowers once they have finished.

Propagation
From semi-ripe stem cuttings taken in summer to fall.

Rhododendron 'Kaponga'

Rhododendron (syn. *Azalea*)
Azalea, rhododendron

FAMILY: Ericaceae
hardiness rating: 6–10

Azaleas are classified in the same genus as rhododendrons, even though they have different common names. There is a huge range of both deciduous and evergreen forms. The name *rhododendron* means rose tree, in reference to the flowers.

Rhododendrons are like other members of the Ericaceae family, preferring acidic soils. Peat or pine needles as a mulch can be used along with an acidic fertilizer to maintain the correct soil pH.

The evergreen forms prefer good light without intense sun, which can burn the leaves or flowers. The deciduous azaleas prefer cooler conditions. Good drainage, shelter from strong winds and moisture over summer are essential for all members of this genus.

Because rhododendrons have a fibrous root system, they can be easily transplanted. The old saying that they like a wheelbarrow ride applies to these plants and camellias.

Pruning

Rhododendrons usually need little pruning if planted in the correct conditions. Deadhead after flowering, using your finger and thumb. If a plant becomes leggy and flowers only on its upper part, cut it back by one-half to one-third. Prune back to existing lower lateral branches.

Some rhododendrons are leggy by nature, such as *Rhododendron* 'Fragrantissimum'. Prune back to a healthy node to encourage bushiness.

Azaleas can be pruned back after flowering to encourage bushiness and a compact shape. If using pruning shears, cut back to nodes behind the flower, or trim lightly with hedge clippers to create an even shape.

Propagation

For evergreen azaleas and rhododendrons, semi-ripe stem cuttings taken from summer through to fall. Deciduous azaleas are propagated from softwood cuttings in spring.

Ribes
Currant

FAMILY: GROSSULARIACEAE

hardiness rating: 5–9

These evergreen and deciduous shrubs come from the Northern Hemisphere. The name *ribes* is derived from an Arab word for rhubarb. The fruiting currants and gooseberries are the most common plants in this genus, but there are ornamental plants. *R. sanguineum* (flowering currant) is a well-known pink-blossomed plant for a border or an informal hedge.

Both ornamental and fruiting currants (*R. nigrum*, blackcurrant, *R. rubrum*, red and white currants and *R. uva-crispa*, gooseberry) are very frost hardy, and need full sun and well-drained soils. Gooseberries seldom fruit well in frost-free climates. Many cultivars are available, including 'Invicta', an early ripener, and the vigorous 'Leveller'.

Ribes sanguineum 'Albidum'

Pruning

Using secateurs (pruning shears), cut back the older shoots of the flowering currants to 1–2 in. (2.5–5 cm) after the blooms are over. Fruiting types should be tackled as follows.

- *R. nigrum* (blackcurrants): This currant bears fruit on new growth so needs hard pruning to encourage new growth and flowering. When planting, prune back all growth to within 2 in. (5 cm) of ground level to encourage strong new growth. Shoots that have fruited should be removed. You can do this pruning when you harvest your crop.
- *R. rubrum* (red and white currants): These currants differ from blackcurrants in that they fruit on two- and three-year-old spurs. Therefore, growth that is one, two or three years old should be left. In late winter or early spring, remove older wood and weak growth to the base with pruning shears and cut back the leader growth by one-half to a node.

Ribes uva-crispa

- *R. uva-crispa* (gooseberries): At planting, six or eight strong leaders should be selected. Cut back these branches by one-half to a node with upward-facing buds. The following winter the leaders can be cut back by one-half again. After that, pruning to remove the 3 Ds is all that is needed.

Propagation
From hardwood stem cuttings taken in winter. Place cuttings directly in the ground, as long as it is free-draining.

Robinia pseudoacacia

Robinia
Robinia
FAMILY: FABACEAE

hardiness rating: 4–10

These fast-growing, deciduous trees are native to the United States and Mexico, and are named after Jean Robin, a French herbalist. They make attractive specimen trees with slightly fragrant flowers and long fruit pods, but some species have spines. They also sucker freely, which can be ideal to stabilize hillsides, but care is needed in smaller gardens.

Robinia hispida (bristly locust, rose acacia) is a thornless shrub reaching 3–5 ft. (1–1.5 m) that has beautiful rose flowers. *R. kelseyi* (syn. *R. hispida* var. *kelseyi*) is a thornless shrub growing to 8 ft. (2.4 m). *R. pseudoacacia* (black locust) is a thorny tree that grows to 70–80 ft. (21–25 m) and is used on farms, but the smaller golden-yellow form, *R. pseudoacacia* 'Frisia', is used ornamentally.

Robinias are cold hardy to –4°F (–20°C), and are tolerant of heat, drought and air pollution.

Pruning Ψ
If planted in a location with adequate room, these trees should need little pruning, other than removal of the 3 Ds. *R. pseudoacacia* 'Frisia' can be crown-raised to improve access, and longer branches shortened back to a suitable lateral branch with pruning saws. Use gloves if pruning the thorny types.

Propagation
From seed that has been soaked, or by grafting for the cultivars.

Rosa
Rose
FAMILY: ROSACEAE

hardiness rating: 2–11

The subject of roses could occupy a whole book. Roses have been cultivated for hundreds of years and there are many different groups in cultivation now. You can broadly classify roses according to whether they are old or modern and by their growth habit.

Old roses include such types as gallicas, damasks, China roses and Bourbon roses. Modern roses include hybrid tea roses, rugosas and floribundas. Roses have a variety of growth habits, including bush, standard, climbers, ramblers, groundcovers and miniatures. They generally need full sun, good drainage and moisture over summer.

Pruning

There is a great deal of mystique regarding the pruning of roses, but it is not difficult and the aim is to improve flowering, plant vigor and health.

Most roses need regular pruning to keep them flowering well over many years and here are some general principles to bear in mind:

- The main pruning should take place once the frosts have past. This is because pruning stimulates rapid new growth, which is susceptible to frost damage. Also, the later you prune, the quicker the regrowth and sealing of wounds.
- Cut into healthy wood, to an outward-facing bud with a slanting cut. Remove all dead and damaged wood.
- Deadheading, or the removal of faded flowers over summer, helps to stimulate further flowering. Cut back to a node past the flower.
- Remove any growth coming from below the bud union where the cultivar was budded on to the rootstock. This is because these suckers are very vigorous and will compete with the desirable growth.
- The main tools you will need are sharp, clean pruning shears and pruning saws. They need to be sharp to get a neat, clean cut to prevent the spread of disease.

Rosa 'Dublin Bay'

As there is such a huge range of roses, only the most common ones are dealt with here.

- *Hybrid tea roses:* These popular roses have long-stemmed flowers and long, pointed buds. They are grown as bushes, standards and climbers. As they bloom on new growth, hard pruning is needed to stimulate new growth. Some rose growers prune harder than others, but as a guideline remove between one-half to one-third of the growth. Remove all weak and inward-growing branches. Older canes that have become woody can be removed if there are adequate new healthy canes. Cut back desired canes to outward-facing buds. Standards can be pruned to create a bowl shape with an open center.
- *Floribunda and polyantha roses:* Floribundas are grown as bushes, standards or climbers; polyanthas are bush roses. Flowers are produced at the tips, with polyanthas having smaller but more flowers (polyantha means many flowers.) These roses do not need to be pruned as hard as hybrid teas. Remove about one-third of the growth.
- *Climbers:* For climbing hybrid tea and floribunda roses, young plants are best left unpruned for two years until the canes are established on the support structure. During the first and second year, removing the 3 Ds is the main priority. In the following years, cut back the laterals to a node, leaving two to three buds. Canes older than four

129

years should be removed to the base as long as there are new canes coming on.

- *Ramblers:* Ramblers produce strong-growing shoots that flower in the second year, and are then removed as they cease to be productive, unlike climbers, which produce long-lived flowering stems. Ramblers should have the flowering stems cut back immediately to their base after flowering in summer.
- *Miniatures:* These are becoming increasingly popular. The main task is to remove dead and diseased material. They generally need only light pruning back to nodes using pruning shears; however, if you cut between nodes it will not harm them as they have so many buds. If some shoots are very vigorous, cut to a node to balance the shape of the plant.
- *Groundcovers:* These roses have also become very popular. They can be trimmed to keep them compact. Use pruning shears to cut back to nodes, although they are often cut back with hedge clippers.

Propagation
From softwood stem cuttings for miniatures, or by budding on to rootstock for hybrid tea roses.

Rosmarinus officinalis 'Prostratus'

Rosmarinus officinalis
Rosemary

FAMILY: Lamiaceae

hardiness rating: 7–10

This aromatic, evergreen shrub is from the Mediterranean. The genus is named for the Latin word, *ros*, dew or moisture, and *marinus*, meaning of the sea, in reference to it growing near the sea. There are prostrate cultivars such as *Rosmarinus officinalis* 'Lockwood de Forest', and upright ones such as *R. officinalis* 'Tuscan Blue', which grows to 6 ft. (1.8 m), and can be trained as a hedge.

Rosemary tolerates hot sun and infertile soils as long as they are well-drained. It is frost hardy to 14°F (–10°C).

Pruning
Cut back the upright cultivars after flowering to maintain a bushy growth habit, and reduce woodiness. Cut back by about one-third with hedge clippers. If growing as a hedge, trim twice a year with hedge clippers. Keep prostrate cultivars bushy and compact by removing the tip growth with pruning shears or hedge clippers.

Propagation
Usually from stem cuttings.

Rubus fruticosus, R. idaeus
Blackberry, bramble, raspberry

FAMILY: ROSACEAE
hardiness rating: 3–9

These deciduous members of the rose family come from Europe are well known for their tasty fruit. The stems producing flowers and fruit are called canes. They need full sun, good drainage and tolerate lime. There are also ornamental shrubs and climbers in this genus.

Pruning

- *Rubus fruticosus* (blackberry, bramble): Fruit is borne on laterals that grow from stems produced the previous year. Plants are usually trained horizontally on wires. Remove the canes that have fruited and tie the new canes, which are produced from the base of the plant, on to the supporting structure.
- *R. idaeus* (raspberry): *Fall fruiting:* Fruit is borne on the current season's growth. The upright growth is cut back to above ground level in late winter–early spring. The new canes will fruit in early fall.
  Summer fruiting: Fruit is borne on last year's canes. In the first season, canes are tied to the wire support. In winter, the top growth is removed back to a node near the top wire. In fall, cut all fruited canes to ground level and tie in the new canes.

Rubus fruticosus

Propagation
From semi-ripe stem cuttings taken in summer or hardwood stem cuttings in winter.

Rubus idaeus 'Heritage'

Ruscus aculeatus
Box holly, butcher's broom

FAMILY: LILIACEAE
hardiness rating: 7–9

This evergreen shrub comes from Southern Europe and North Africa. The name *ruscus* comes from the Latin word for butcher's broom, referring to the use of the branches by butchers for sweeping. *Aculeatus* means armed with prickles, in reference to the spine-tipped cladodes, which are stems that function as leaves. The attractive red berries are more reliable in *Ruscus aculeatus* 'Wheelers Variety'.

The shrub will grow in dry, shady locations, but will also tolerate full sun.

Pruning
Remove dead or spindly stems back to their base in spring using a pruning saw. Use gloves when handling the stems.

Propagation
From seed or division.

Ruscus aculeatus

Salix caprea 'Pendula'

Salix
Willow

FAMILY: Salicaceae

hardiness rating: 2 –9

These plants come from the Northern Hemisphere and are mainly deciduous. The name *salix* comes from the Latin word for willow.

- *Salix babylonica* (weeping willow) is a well-known tree found beside rivers, growing up to 50 ft. (15 m) in height.
- *S. caprea* 'Pendula' (syn. *S. caprea* 'Kilmarnock', Kilmarnock willow) is almost always grown as a grafted standard. It can reach 6 ft. (2 m) or more, depending on the height of the graft.
- *S. magnifica* is a smaller tree, at 15 ft. (5 m), with attractive leaves.
- *S. matsudana* 'Tortuosa' (syn. *S. babylonica* var. *pekinensis* 'Tortuosa', corkscrew willow, dragon-claw willow) has unusual twisted branches and makes a lovely specimen tree. It grows to 50 ft. (15 m).

Willows prefer damp sites, making them a favorite near streams. However, due to their invasive root system, they block drains, so keep them well away if in any doubt about the soundness of your drains.

Pruning Ψ

As a specimen, willows should not need pruning if planted in the correct location, but may need dead and damaged wood removed. The lower weeping branches can be cut off to prevent them reaching the ground and making access difficult. Prune back to a collar with a pruning saw, undercutting the branches first. Watch out for any branches under tension as they can spring back and hit you.

Propagation

From hardwood stem cuttings taken in winter. Like poplars, willows can be started with large pieces of stem, up to 6 ft. (1.8 m) long, buried about 12 in. (30 cm) into the ground, where they will root freely.

Salvia officinalis

Salvia
Sage

FAMILY: Lamiaceae

hardiness rating: 3–11

This genus includes many species of annuals, herbaceous perennials and soft-wooded shrubs with a very wide distribution. The name comes from the Latin word *salvus*, meaning safe or well, referring to the supposed healing properties of *Salix officinalis* (common sage, purple sage). Some perennial sages include *S. farinacea* (mealycup sage), which has blue flowers, and grows to 2–3 ft. (60–90 cm). *S. fulgens* (syn. *S. cardinalis*) grows to 2 ft. 6 in. (75 cm), and has scarlet flowers. *S. microphylla* (syn. *S. grahamii*) forms a shrub 12–24 in. (30–60 cm) high with red flowers.

S. officinalis grows to 2 ft. 6 in. (75 cm), and *S. patens* (gentian sage) grows to 24 in. (60 cm). Both have blue flowers. There are many cultivars, such as *S.* 'Summer Skies'.

Species such as *S. officinalis* are frost hardy, while species from Mexico and South America tolerate only light frosts. These sages all need full sun and a free-draining soil.

Pruning

S. officinalis can be cut back in early spring to create new growth. Use pruning shears, and cut back the plant by about one-third to nodes. Other species should be deadheaded after flowering by cutting back to a node past the spent flowers with pruning shears.

Propagation

From seed for the species, and by division or stem cuttings for the cultivars and hybrids.

Santolina

FAMILY: Asteraceae
hardiness rating: 6–10

These aromatic shrubs and herbaceous perennials are from the Mediterranean. The name comes from the Latin *sanctus linum*, meaning holy flax. They have silvery-gray foliage, and yellow flowers in summer, and are ideal for hot, dry banks.

Santolina chamaecyparissus (syn. *S. incana*, lavender cotton) grows to 18 in. (45 cm). *S. pinnata* (syn. *S. chamaecyparissus* subsp. *tomentosa*) grows to 18–30 in. (45–75 cm), while *S. rosmarinifolia* (syn. *S. virens*, *S. viridis*, holy flax) grows to 24 in. (60 cm).

These shrubs all need a free-draining, limey soil and full sun, and are frost hardy.

Santolia chamaecyparissus

Pruning

Cut old stems back to the base with pruning shears immediately after flowering to encourage new growth. In fall deadhead plants by removing the old flowerheads and stalks with pruning shears or hedge clippers.

Propagation

From seed or stem cuttings.

Sarcococca
Christmas box, sweet box

FAMILY: Buxaceae
hardiness rating: 6–10

These evergreen, fragrant shrubs are native to Asia. The name comes from the Greek *sarkos*, flesh, and *kokos*, a berry, in reference to the fleshy fruits. They have fragrant late winter flowers, fruit over summer, and lush green leaves year round. They are ideally planted in shady areas in groups.

Sarcococca confusa grows to 6 ft. (1.8 m), *S. hookeriana* to 3 ft. (1 m), and the more popular *S. ruscifolia* to 4 ft. (1.2 m). The plants grow in cool shady conditions, and need a free-draining, slightly acidic soil.

Sarcococca ruscifolia

133

Pruning
Little pruning is required other than the removal of the 3 Ds.

Propagation
From stratified seed or by stem cuttings.

Schinus molle

Schinus
Pepper tree

FAMILY: ANACARDIACEAE

hardiness rating: 9–11

The evergreen trees and shrubs in this genus are from Central and South America. The name comes from the Greek *schinos*, the mastic tree, referring to the resinous juices that some species have. The common name pepper tree refers to the pungent red fruit, although they are not used for pepper. *Schinus molle* (pepper tree, Peruvian mastic tree) has aromatic leaves, and grows 30–50 ft. (9–15 m). *S. terebinthifolius* (Brazilian pepper tree, Christmasberry tree) grows up to 30 ft. (9 m).

Pepper trees grow to maturity very quickly, and can become weeds in warmer climates. They tolerate drought conditions, and light frosts.

Pruning Ψ
These trees can be crown-raised if access is needed underneath. Cut back lower branches to their collar with a pruning saw. Make sure there is adequate room for these trees to grow, as they have a spreading growth habit.

Propagation
From seed or stem cuttings.

Sequoia sempervirens
California redwood, coast redwood

FAMILY: TAXODIACEAE

hardiness rating: 8–9

These long-lived, very tall evergreen conifers are from coastal California and Oregon. The name *Sequoia* refers to Sequoiah, creator of the Cherokee alphabet. *Sempervirens* is Greek for evergreen. The whole tree has a resinous aroma, like pine wood. A redwood is the world's tallest recorded tree, at 364 ft. (111 m), but there are cultivars that are a manageable size, such as *S. sempervirens* 'Adpressa', which eventually grows to 20 ft. (6 m).

The redwood is tolerant of a range of climatic conditions, but needs adequate moisture when young.

Pruning Ψ
The suckers at the base of the tree should be removed back to the collar with a pruning saw. As it is a large tree, it needs adequate space to grow. Cultivars require pruning when young to obtain a good form.

Sequoia sempervirens

Propagation

From seed, or from stem cuttings for the cultivars.

Skimmia japonica

FAMILY: RUTACEAE
hardiness rating: 6–9

This evergreen shrub is native to Japan, China and Southeast Asia. It has fragrant white flowers in spring, followed by red berries that last into winter. As this species has male and female plants, you need both to produce berries.

The plant grows well with rhododendrons and camellias, preferring shade or part-shade, and a soil rich in organic matter.

Skimmia japonica

Pruning

Little pruning is required, other than removal of the 3 Ds.

Propagation

From stem cuttings.

Sophora
Kowhai

FAMILY: FABACEAE
hardiness rating: 7–10

Evergreen and deciduous trees and shrubs in this genus are found throughout the world, but are commonly known as kowhai, from the New Zealand species. *Sophora* comes from an Arabic word for a legume, while the name *kowhai* means yellow in the Maori language.

Sophora microphylla and *S. tetraptera* are taller trees from New Zealand, growing to 20 ft. (6 m), while *S. prostrata* is a small shrub. The trees make ideal specimens, their fern-like foliage and yellow flowers creating a majestic sight in spring.

S. japonica (Japanese pagoda tree) is a deciduous tree with white flowers that grows to 20 ft. (6 m).

Kowhai naturally grow near rivers, lakes or other moist areas, and can grow in the sun or shade.

Sophora microphylla

Pruning Ψ

Kowhai seldom need pruning, other than removal of the 3 Ds. Care should be taken with the cuts, as the bark tears easily. They generally don't require crown-raising as they naturally form a clean trunk lower down.

Propagation

From seed that has been soaked in hot water before sowing.

Sorbus aucuparia

Sorbus

FAMILY: ROSACEAE

hardiness rating: 3–9

These deciduous trees and shrubs from Europe and Asia are named from the Latin *sorbum*, meaning serviceberry. They have attractive flowers, rich fall foliage and colorful fruit.

- *Sorbus americana* (American mountain ash, dogberry) grows to 30 ft. (9 m), is very frost hardy, and has red berries.
- *S. aria* (whitebeam) grows to 30 ft. (9 m).
- *S. aucuparia* (European mountain ash, rowan) is the most commonly grown species, growing to 50 ft. (15 m). It is very frost hardy, and has orange berries.
- *S. cashmiriana* grows to 25 ft. (7.6 m), and has white berries.
- *S. hupehensis* (syn. *S. glabrescens*, Hubei mountain ash) grows to 50 ft. (15 m) and has white berries.
- *S. reducta* is a small, suckering shrub growing to 5 ft. (1.5 m), with carmine fruit.
- *S. terminalis* grows to 50 ft. (15 m), and has reddish-brown fruit.

Sorbus grow well where there is a dry fall and cold winter. Plant them in full sun and provide adequate moisture over dry periods.

Pruning Ψ

Little pruning is required other than forming a good leader and clear trunk. *S. aria* needs training to form a clear trunk to 6 ft. (1.8 m), while the other species form clear trunks. Lower branches can be removed back to the collar, using a pruning saw.

Propagation

From stratified seed, or cultivars by layering.

Spiraea x arguta

Spiraea

Spirea

FAMILY: ROSACEAE

hardiness rating: 4–9

These hardy, deciduous shrubs come from the Northern Hemisphere. The name comes from *speiraia*, a Greek word for a plant used for garlands. They are ideal as fillers with other spring-flowering plants.

There are two types:

- Those with white flowers produced from last year's growth. This includes *Spiraea* x *arguta* (bridal wreath, foam of May), *S.* x *cinerea* 'Grefsheim', *S. nipponica* and *S.* x *vanhouttei* (Van Houtte spirea).
- Those producing pink or red flowers on the current year's growth. This includes *S. japonica* (Japanese spirea), a popular species with many cultivars, and *S. douglasii*.

Spireas are very hardy, growing in most soils and in sun or partial shade.

Pruning

Those that flower on last year's growth need lighter pruning after flowering. Cut back to a node past the spent flower with pruning shears.

Those that flower on the current year's growth need harder pruning to encourage new growth. They can be cut down to within 4 in. (10 cm) of the ground with pruning shears after flowering.

Propagation

From semi-ripe stem cuttings taken in fall, or hardwood stem cuttings taken in winter.

Stachyurus praecox

FAMILY: STACHYURACEAE
hardiness rating: 7–9

This hardy deciduous shrub, native to Japan, is named from the Greek *stachys*, a spike, and *oura*, a tail, referring to the shape of the flowers. It has impressive flowers from late winter through to early spring, and is ideal against a sunny wall.

It prefers a free-draining, slightly acidic soil with adequate moisture over dry periods, and grows in sun or semi-shade.

Stachyurus praecox

Pruning

If trained against a wall, remove stems that come out from the wall in favor of those that are growing along the wall. Remove any deadwood and spindly stems back to ground level after flowering.

Propagation

From stem cuttings.

Stenocarpus sinuatus
Firewheel tree

FAMILY: PROTEACEAE
hardiness rating: 8

This evergreen tree from coastal Queensland is named after the Greek *stenos*, narrow, and *karpos*, fruit, in reference to the almost flat follicles or seed capsules. *Sinuatus* means with a wavy margin, referring to the leaves. The tree has attractive foliage and orange-red flowers in late summer and fall.

It needs a sunny, warm location free of frosts, and an acidic soil.

Pruning

Early training involves removing lower branches to get a single clear trunk. Young trees can be grown in containers, and kept bushy by cutting stems back to nodes to obtain the desired shape and size.

Propagation

From seed or cuttings.

Stenocarpus sinuatus

Stewartia pseudocamellia

Stewartia

FAMILY: Theaceae

hardiness rating: 5–9

These deciduous trees and shrubs from Eastern North America and Eastern Asia are related to camellias. They are named after John Stuart, an 18th-century patron of horticulture. They are noted for their fall leaf color, ornamental bark and summer flowers.

Stewartia pseudocamellia (Japanese stewartia) from Japan normally grows to 20 ft. (6 m). *S. sinensis* from China grows to 30 ft. (9 m).

Like camellias, they grow well in woodland conditions; that is, in semi-shade and in an acidic soil high in organic matter.

Pruning

Little pruning is needed, unless access is needed under the tree, in which case the crown can be raised.

Propagation

From seed or stem cuttings.

Styrax japonica

Styrax japonica
Japanese snowbell

FAMILY: Styracaceae

hardiness rating: 6–8

This beautiful deciduous small tree is native to China and Japan. *Styrax* is a classical Greek name, while *japonica* means from Japan. From late spring to mid-summer the tree bears hanging fragrant flowers, which can be best seen from below, so plant in an elevated position.

The Japanese snowball prefers to be shaded from the hot sun, and is cold hardy to 5°F (–15°C). Grow the tree in a slightly acidic soil with adequate moisture during dry periods.

Pruning

Little pruning is needed other than removal of the 3 Ds and lower branches back to the collar.

Propagation

From stratified seed.

Symphoricarpos orbiculatus

Symphoricarpos
Snowberry

FAMILY: Caprifoliaceae

hardiness rating: 2–10

These deciduous shrubs are mostly natives of North America. They are named from the Greek *symphorein*, bear together, and *carpos*, fruit, in reference to the attractive clustered fruit.

Symphoricarpos albus var. *laevigatus* (syn. *S. rivularis*, snowberry) is a suckering shrub growing to 6 ft. (1.8 m) with white berries, while *S. orbiculatus* (coralberry, Indian currant) grows to the same height and has pink berries.

Snowberries tolerate shade, poor soils and air pollution, so make good plants for city gardens.

Pruning
S. albus var. *laevigatus* forms suckers, which can be dug out or left to spread if there is room.

Remove weak and overcrowded shoots in late winter back to the collar with a pruning saw.

Propagation
From stem cuttings taken in late fall-winter.

Syringa vulgaris
Common lilac, French lilac

FAMILY: OLEACEAE

hardiness rating: 4–8

The spring-flowering deciduous trees and shrubs of this genus are from Asia and Europe. The botanical name comes from the Greek word *syrinx*, a pipe or tube, and refers to the long, tube-like flowers. Lilacs are ideal among other evergreen shrubs and spring-flowering plants. Many of the garden favorites have been developed from hybrids of *Syringa vulgaris*, including both single- and double-flowering forms.

Lilacs prefer alkaline soil, so add lime around the plants. Grow in sun or shade with adequate moisture over summer.

Syringa vulgaris 'Alphonse Lavelle'

Pruning
The *vulgaris* lilacs flower from buds formed the previous season. The leaf buds develop just below these flower buds. It is a good idea to remove spent flowers, but avoid damaging the new growth below, as this will produce next year's flowers. Cut back past the spent flowers with pruning shears to the nearest node. Old or unshapely plants can be cut back to nodes about 2–3 ft. (60–90 cm) above ground level.

They usually make good regrowth but will take two years to produce flowers.

Propagation
From hardwood stem cuttings taken in winter or from suckers removed from the plant. Selected forms are grafted, usually on to the rootstock of the common privet.

Tamarix
Tamarisk

FAMILY: TAMARICACEAE

hardiness rating: 3–9

These deciduous trees and shrubs are from Asia and Europe. *Tamarix* is a Latin name meaning salt cedar. *Tamarix juniperina* (syn. *T. chinensis, T. elegans*) and *T. pentandra* (syn. *T. ramosissima*, five-stamen tamarisk) are two common species, both growing to 10 to 15 ft. (3–5 m). Both are also popular

Tamarix gallica

as bonsai specimens. *T. gallica* (salt cedar, French tamarisk) reaches 20 ft. (6 m) and like many tamarisk species, can be an invasive plant in some regions. Tamarisks have fine leaves and masses of pink flowers in spring and summer.

Growing naturally around coastlines, often in very salty soils, these plants tolerate very dry, hot conditions, which makes them ideal for background planting in seaside gardens.

Pruning

Tamarisks have a very open, spreading growth habit and regular pruning will keep them compact. When planting or transplanting, they should be cut back to within 12 in. (30 cm) of the ground with loppers or pruning shears.

Pruning depends on the time of flowering:

- Tamarisks that flower in early spring, such as *T. juniperina*, have flowers on growth produced the previous year. They should therefore be cut back as soon as the blooms fade. Cut back by about one-third to a node using pruning shears.
- Tamarisks that flower in summer, such as *T. pentandra*, have flowers produced on current growth. They can be cut back hard in winter to encourage new growth and keep the plant compact and free-flowering. Cut them to within 12 in. (30 cm) of the ground with loppers or pruning saw.

Propagation
From hardwood stem cuttings taken in winter.

Taxodium distichum

Taxodium distichum
FAMILY: TAXODIACEAE
Bald cypress, swamp cypress
hardiness rating: 5–10

This deciduous tree from Southeastern United States grows in rivers and coastal swamp areas. The name *taxodium* comes from the Greek *taxus*, the yew, and *eidos*, resembling, due to the resemblance to yew. *Distichum* means in two ranks, referring to the leaf arrangement. Swamp cypresses have unique buttressed trunks and woody projections known as cypress knees, which are thought to assist aeration of submerged roots.

They are hardy trees, preferring moist soils, and ideal near waterways.

Pruning Ψ
No regular pruning is required other than the removal of 3 Ds.

Propagation
From seed.

Taxus baccata
English yew

FAMILY: TAXACEAE
hardiness rating: 7–8

Taxus baccata

This evergreen conifer is found in Western Asia, North Africa and Europe. There are specimens in England that are centuries old, often used as hedges and for topiary.

Taxus baccata can grow to 50 ft. (15 m), although the cultivars are generally smaller. *T. baccata* 'Fastigiata' (Irish yew) is a columnar tree that grows to 30–50 ft. (9–15 m), while *T. baccata* 'Adpressa' is a spreading shrub that can reach 20 ft. (6 m).

Yews tolerate a range of conditions, including shade and alkaline soils, but do not grow well where summers are hot and dry.

Pruning Ψ

Little pruning is necessary. Columnar types such as *T. baccata* 'Fastigiata' may have branch fallout. Prune them in summer to maintain a neat outline with pruning shears. Prune only the recent growth back to a node or collar, because if you prune back too hard you will get dieback.

Propagation

From stratified seed or stem cuttings in summer or winter.

Telopea
Waratah

FAMILY: PROTEACEAE
hardiness rating: 10–11

Telopea speciosissima
'Flaming Beacon'

These evergreen shrubs from Australia are named after the Greek word *telopos*, meaning seen from afar, in reference to the very visible flowers. The common name waratah is an Aboriginal name also meaning 'seen from afar'.

Telopea oreades (Grippsland waratah, Victorian waratah) grows to 20–27 ft. (6–8 m), and has red flowers. *T. speciosissima* (common waratah, New South Wales waratah, Sydney waratah) grows to 10 ft. (3 m) tall, and has brilliant coral red or crimson-scarlet flowers in spring and summer. The species name *speciosissima* means most beautiful.

Waratahs need a free-draining, slightly acidic soil, shelter from strong winds and are cold hardy to 23°F (–5°C).

Pruning

Remove the tips of young plants back to a node using pruning shears to encourage bushiness and flowering. When cutting flowers for display, cut back to a node with pruning shears, and after flowering cut any old flowered stems half-way back to a node. Don't cut back too hard into old wood, as it won't regenerate.

Propagation

From seed that has been scarified or soaked.

141

Teucrium fruticans

Teucrium
Germander

FAMILY: LAMIACEAE
hardiness rating: 5–10

These evergreen shrubs and herbs are from Asia and the Mediterranean. The name comes from the Greek *Teucer*, a warrior from Troy who is said to have used the plant medicinally.

The main plant grown is *Teucrium fruticans* (shrubby germander, silver germander, tree germander). It has silvery leaves and blue flowers, and is ideal as a hedge or as a contrast to plants with brighter red or purple foliage. It grows to about 6 ft. (1.8 m). *T. chamaedrys* (wall germander) grows to 8 in. (20 cm).

Like many silver plants, germanders enjoy hot, dry coastal conditions with free-draining soils.

Pruning

Because of their rapid growth these plants need regular trimming with hedge clippers. *T. chamaedrys* can be cut back in spring to keep it as a groundcover. Cut back *T. fruticans* after flowering. In warmer climates, it can be pruned three or four times per year, by cutting the long shoots back to the denser growth with hedge clippers.

If shoots are damaged by frost they should be cut back in spring when frosts are finished.

Propagation
From seed or stem cuttings.

Thryptomene calycina

Thryptomene
Heath myrtle

FAMILY: MYRTACEAE
hardiness rating: 9–11

These evergreen shrubs from Western Australia are named from the Greek *thrypto*, meaning to break into pieces, referring to the fact that the flowers fall readily. They have aromatic leaves and fragrant flowers, which are ideal for cutting.

Thryptomene calycina has white flowers, while *T. oreades* has pink flowers.

They need an acidic soil, and will grow in full sun or partial shade.

Pruning
Young plants can have their growing tips removed to encourage bushiness. When cutting flowers, cut back with pruning shears to a node past the flower stem. At the end of flowering, cut back all growth past the flowers with pruning shears or hedge clippers.

Propagation
From seed or stem cuttings.

*Thuja (*syn. *Platycladus)*
Arborvitae

FAMILY: CUPRESSACEAE

hardiness rating: 5–9

These evergreen conifers are from North America, China and Japan. The name *thuja* is from the Greek *thuia*, and its origin is thought to mean sacrifice, referring to the resin used for incense. The common name *arborvitae* means tree of life. These conifers are noted for having flattened foliage and a strong, fruity scent when the leaves are crushed.

Thuja occidentalis (American arborvitae, white cedar) is from Eastern United States while *T. plicata* (Western red cedar) is from Western United States. *T. orientalis* (syn. *Biota orientalis, Platycladus orientalis*, oriental arborvitae) is from China and Japan. *T. occidentalis* can grow to 60 ft. (18 m), *T. orientalis* to 40 ft. (12 m). *T. plicata* can grow to 200 ft. (60 m). These species have provided many cultivars, which are used ornamentally. The species are used largely for commercial forestry purposes.

The conifers are tolerant of most conditions, preferring full sun and adequate moisture during dry periods.

Thuja occidentalis 'Fastigiata'

Pruning Ψ

Little pruning is required, as even the smaller cultivars hold their form well. The spreading branches can break under snow, so you can reduce the length of the longest branches by pruning back to a suitable lateral branch, as long as it doesn't affect the appearance of the tree. If branches do break, cut them back to the collar.

Propagation

From seed or by stem cuttings.

Thymus
Thyme

FAMILY: LAMIACEAE

hardiness rating: 4–9

These evergreen prostrate and mound-forming herbaceous perennials are from Asia and Southern Europe. They have aromatic leaves, and are used for both culinary and ornamental purposes, where they are ideal in rockeries and on banks.

Thymus serpyllum (mother of thyme, serpolet, wild thyme) grows to 1–2 in (2.5–5 cm) high, while *T. vulgaris* (common thyme, garden thyme) grows 6–12 in (15–30 cm). *T. x citriodorus* (lemon-scented thyme, lemon thyme) grows to 12 in. (30 cm), and as both the specific and common name suggest, it has a strong lemon scent.

These plants thrive in a sunny area with well-drained soils.

Thymus serpyllum

Pruning

After flowering, cut back beyond the old flower heads with pruning shears or hedge clippers.

Propagation

From seed, layering or from stem cuttings.

Tilia
FAMILY: TILIACEAE

Lime tree, linden
hardiness rating: 3–9

These tall, deciduous trees with fragrant flowers come from North America, Europe and Asia. The name comes from the Latin *tilia*, meaning linden or lime tree.

- *Tilia americana* (American linden, basswood) grows to 120 ft. (36 m) with a straight trunk and corky bark.
- *T. cordata* (little-leaf linden) can grow to 100 ft. (30 m), but usually smaller in cultivation.
- *T.* x *europaea* (syn. *T. intermedia*, *T.* x *vulgaris*, European linden) can grow to 100 ft. (30 m), but is prone to aphid infestation, which causes an unsightly black on the leaves. It also forms suckers.
- *T. platyphyllos* (large-leaved linden) is a European species growing to 80 ft. (25 m), and forms suckers.
- *T. tomentosa* (European white linden, silver linden) grows to 90 ft. (27 m).

Tilia are tolerant of air pollution, and prefer hot summers and cold winters. Plant them in a well-drained soil and provide moisture over dry periods.

Tilia x *europaea*

Pruning Ψ

These trees can be pleached or kept pruned to a smaller size for street planting. If you allow them to grow to their natural size, train them to a single leader by removing any competing upright lateral branches. It is preferable to prune them over the summer period to allow the wound to seal and to more readily identify deadwood for removal. You can remove the suckers in *T.* x *europaea* and *T. platyphyllos* back to their base with a pruning saw.

Propagation

From seed or by layering or grafting for the cultivars.

Toona sinensis (syn. *Cedrela sinensis*)
FAMILY: MELIACEAE

Chinese toon
hardiness rating: 6–9

This deciduous tree from China and Southeast Asia was previously known as *Cedrela sinensis*. The specific name means from China. It has aromatic timber, and attractive pink new foliage, especially in *Toona sinensis* 'Flamingo'. It can grow as a single stem, but as it suckers, it can often form a clump of stems. These can grow to 30 ft. (9 m). The bark can cause skin irritations.

Toon trees prefer full sun, shelter and a soil with adequate moisture.

Toona sinensis 'Flamingo'

Pruning

They can be crown-reduced by cutting back to suitable lateral branches. Suckers can be cut back to ground level with a pruning saw.

Propagation

From seed or by root cuttings.

Trachelospermum jasminoides
Star jasmine

FAMILY: APOCYNACEAE

hardiness rating: 8–11

This species from China is the most commonly grown of the 20 or so evergreen climbers in this genus. The generic name comes from the Greek *trachelos*, neck, and *sperma*, seed. The species name *jasminoides* means resembling jasmine, as the flowers are similar. It has very fragrant, white, starry flowers from late spring to summer. It includes cultivars such as *Trachelospermum jasminoides* 'Variegatum'.

Star jasmine will grow in sun or partial shade.

Pruning

Star jasmine needs to be trained initially along a structure such as trellis or wires. In fall, growth that is weak or coming out from the main growth can be cut back to a collar with pruning shears or pruning saws.

Trachelospermum jasminoides

Propagation

From seed or from stem cuttings in summer in the case of varieties.

Tsuga
Hemlock

FAMILY: PINACEAE

hardiness rating: 4–9

These evergreen conifers are from cool temperate areas in North America and East Asia. *Tsuga* is a Japanese name for this tree. The genus includes tall trees and dwarf cultivars.

Tsuga heterophylla

- *Tsuga canadensis* (Canada hemlock) from the Eastern North America can grow to 80 ft. (25 m), while *T. canadensis* 'Pendula' (Sargent's weeping hemlock) grows to at least 6 ft. (1.8 m).
- *T. caroliniana* (Carolina hemlock), from the Appalachians from Virginia to Georgia, grows up to 70 ft. (21 m).
- *T. chinensis* (Chinese hemlock) has been used extensively in cultivation in Japan, where it seldom reaches its natural height of about 70 ft. (21 m).
- *T. heterophylla* (western hemlock) from Western North America (Alaska to California) is a fast-growing, tall tree that can reach to 200 ft. (60 m) in its natural state, and is often used for timber.

Hemlocks are very frost hardy, and can grow in the shade. They prefer a slightly acidic soil.

Pruning Ψ

Little pruning is required as the lower branches reaching the ground are a feature. Make sure you have enough room for the larger species to grow, or if space is limited, use one of the many smaller cultivars.

Propagation

From seed or by stem cuttings for the cultivars.

Ulmus procera

Ulmus
Elm

FAMILY: Ulmaceae

hardiness rating: 3–9

These large deciduous trees come from the Northern Hemisphere. The name *ulmus* is Latin for elm.

Ulmus glabra 'Pendula' (weeping Dutch elm, weeping wych elm) grows to 10 ft. (3 m), making a perfect "umbrella" lawn specimen. *U. procera* 'Louis van Houtte' (golden elm) can grow to 33 ft. (10 m) and has lovely gold leaves. *U. glabra* 'Lutescens' also has golden leaves. *U. parvifolia* (Chinese elm, lacebark elm) is a very hardy tree reaching up to 50 ft. (15 m).

Elms will tolerate wind, but need moisture to get established. Some species, such as *U. procera*, form suckers that crop up wherever there is room to grow.

Most of us are aware of the damaging effect of Dutch elm disease, although some species are resistant to the disease.

Elms transplant relatively easily, even as large specimens.

Pruning Ψ

If planted in the correct location for their size and form, these trees should need little pruning. They should have the 3 Ds removed and their crown can be thinned if more light is needed. However, as they are large trees, this is a job for an arborist. Suckers will need to be continually removed to ground level with a pruning saw. As street trees, they can be cut back each year to control their height, and will grow back rapidly.

Propagation

From hardwood stem cuttings taken in winter. However, the golden and weeping forms are usually grafted.

Umbellularia californica

Umbellularia californica
California laurel, headache tree

FAMILY: Lauraceae

hardiness rating: 7–9

This evergreen tree from California and Oregon is the only species in the genus. Its common name refers to the aromatic leaves, which, when crushed, can cause an instant headache if inhaled. It grows up to 80 ft. (25 m) in height. It is very frost hardy once established, and grows best in full sun with shelter from strong winds. Grow in a free-draining soil with adequate moisture.

Pruning Ψ
Little pruning is required for this tree other than removal of the 3 Ds.

Propagation
From seed in fall.

Vaccinium
Bilberry, blueberry, cranberry, huckleberry

FAMILY: ERICACEAE
hardiness rating: 2–10

Vaccinium delavayi

The evergreen and deciduous shrubs, small trees and climbers of this genus are from the Northern Hemisphere. They are renowned for their leaf color in fall, and edible berries that are red or blue-black. They grow well in the shade and the cold. They need an acidic soil that retains moisture.

- *Vaccinium arboreum* (tree sparkleberry) is a deciduous to semi-deciduous small tree from Southeastern United States.
- *V. delavayi* is a spreading shrub, growing to 24 in. (60 cm). It produces deep red berries and originates from China.
- *V. macrocarpon* (cranberry) is a low-growing plant from Eastern North America. The specific name comes from the Greek *macro*, large, and *karpos*, fruit, referring to the large red fruits.
- *V. myrtillus* (bilberry, sourtop blueberry, whortleberry) is a deciduous shrub from Europe and Asia with blue-black berries.
- *V. ovatum* (box blueberry, California huckleberry) is a shrub from Oregon to south California with red-black berries.
- *V. vitis-idaea* (cowberry) grows to 6–12 in. (15–30 cm), with red berries.

Pruning
The lower-growing species such as *V. macrocarpon* need little pruning other than removal of weak growth in spring back to a node or collar. Larger deciduous trees such as *V. arboreum* can have older weaker growth cut back to the collar with a pruning saw in winter.

Propagation
By seed or division.

Viburnum
Viburnum

FAMILY: CAPRIFOLIACEAE
hardiness rating: 2–9

These evergreen and deciduous shrubs and trees are found in the Northern Hemisphere. There are many species and cultivars grown for their flowers, foliage and berries.

- *Viburnum* x *burkwoodii* grows to 8 ft. (2.4 m) and has fragrant flowers.
- *V. davidii* has blue berries and grows to 3–5 ft. (1–1.5 m).
- *V. opulus* 'Sterile' (syn. 'Roseum', snowball tree) has snowball-like flowers in spring, hence its common name.

Viburnum x *burkwoodii*

- *V. tinus* (laurustinus) has pink flowers and grows to 15 ft. (4.5 m).

Viburnums tolerate the cold and can grow in sun or semi-shade. They prefer soils rich in organic matter, such as peat or compost.

Pruning

Most viburnums need little pruning if grown in the correct location. Shrubby plants like *V. tinus* can be kept trimmed to a neat shape. Cut back after flowering to a node at the required height.

Other plants like *V.* x *burkwoodii* can be pruned in spring after they have flowered. They have a leggy growth habit when young, which can be improved by cutting back to a node past the faded flowers.

Propagation

From seed that has been cooled in the fridge. Otherwise, hardwood stem cuttings can be taken in winter.

Virgilia divaricata

Virgilia divaricata
Keurboom, virgilia

FAMILY: FABACEAE

hardiness rating: 9–11

There are only two species of small trees in this South African genus. The more common one is *Virgilia divaricata*.

The rapid growth of this tree provides a quick screen. Because of its shallow roots, it can blow over in high winds. It is also short-lived, usually lasting for about 15 years. When in full flower in spring and summer keurbooms are a spectacular sight.

Keurbooms prefer full sun, and tolerate dry soil and coastal winds. They often flower more prolifically if grown in harsher conditions.

They are difficult to transplant once over 7–10 ft. (2.1–3 m).

Pruning Ψ

Normally this tree does not need pruning. However, it does develop a lot of deadwood that can be removed along with any damaged wood. It can be crown-raised to allow other plants to grow under it. Prune branches back to the collar with a saw.

Keep the plant denser and more compact by cutting back the new growth to the nearest node during the growing season.

Propagation
From seed.

Vitis
Grape

FAMILY: VITACEAE

hardiness rating: 4–10

These climbers from around the world include fruiting grapevines as well as ornamental grapes. *Vitis amurensis* (Amur grape) is an ornamental with brilliant fall foliage. To grow grapes successfully, especially the fruiting types, you need hot, dry summers to ripen the grapes. The vines are moderately cold hardy and prefer an alkaline soil.

Vitis vinifera

Pruning

Fruiting grapevines are usually trained with a main vertical stem to a selected height from which horizontal arms can spread. Support can be given by running wires between uprights.

Grapevines produce fruit on the current season's growth and pruning encourages this.

The other important factor to consider is timing. Grapevines should be pruned in early winter, after leaf fall. In mid-winter to early spring the sap flow increases very strongly. If grapevines are pruned at this time, the sap can flow from cuts like water from a tap. This can reduce vigor and affect fruit production as well as cause dieback.

The aim in training and pruning grapevines is to establish strong arms from which laterals are produced. These established laterals are then pruned back to two buds each year.

Vitis vinifera 'Chasselas'

Vines need to be securely tied to a support structure. When cutting to a node, do not cut too close to the buds. It usually takes three years to establish a fruiting grapevine.

- *One-year-old vines:* Vines should be left for their first year, after which one strong stem is selected. In winter, cut this stem back to the third node above the ground. In summer, this strong stem can be cut back to the height of the support wire to promote side-branching.
- *Two-year-old vines:* In the second winter, remove all lateral growth arising from the arms. Prune the horizontal arms to a length of about 20–24 in. (50–60 cm) to a downward-facing bud.
- *Three-year-old vines:* In the third winter, select strong laterals at about 12 in. (30 cm) spacing. Weak lateral growth can be removed back to the arms. The selected laterals should be shortened back to two buds each year. In summer, when the fruits are ripening, cut out the tip of each shoot three nodes past the fruit to aid ripening.

Propagation

Fruiting grapevines are usually grafted onto a suitable rootstock.

Weigela florida
Apple blossom

FAMILY: CAPRIFOLIACEAE
hardiness rating: 5–9

This deciduous shrub come from Asia. The name *florida* means flowery and refers to the prolific flowers in spring and summer. *Weigela florida* and its many cultivars and hybrids are commonly grown and flowers are available in pink, red and crimson.

Apple blossoms are excellent in shrub borders with other spring-flowering plants. They are very hardy plants, tolerant of dry conditions

Weigela florida

and wind exposure. Unless the soil is particularly fertile, they may need regular feeding with a general fertilizer.

Pruning

Prune immediately after flowering. Cut back to a node with a strong lateral shoot. Older stems can be cut back to the base with loppers. This will result in rapid regrowth of new shoots. Thin out weaker shoots by removing them to the base. The variegated weigelas can revert to the green form. Cut these green shoots out to the base as soon as they appear.

Propagation

From semi-ripe stem cuttings in summer or longer hardwood cuttings in winter.

Wisteria sinensis

Wisteria
Wisteria

FAMILY: FABACEAE

hardiness rating: 5–9

These deciduous climbers come from Asia and Central and Southern United States. Members of the pea family, they have spectacular flowers that appear before the leaves.

Wisteria floribunda (Japanese wisteria) has fragrant, violet flowers, while another cultivar, *W. floribunda* 'Alba' (syn. 'Shiro Noda'), has white flowers. *W. sinensis* (syn. *W.chinensis*, Chinese wisteria) has fragrant mauve-lilac flowers. The species name *sinensis* means from China.

With age wisterias can develop beautiful, twisted trunks. They are ideal for growing on a pergola, trellis or fence. They like full sun, adequate moisture during the flowering and growth season, and protection from strong winds. They are mostly frost hardy.

Pruning

The aim when training and pruning wisteria is to encourage the main growth along the support structures without tangling, and to keep the long lateral growth contained. The flower spurs that arise from the laterals are then kept near the main stem.

When training young plants, tie the main growths to supports, keeping them apart from each other. In summer, cut back with pruning shears any long trailing growth to a node close to the main stem. In winter, the leader can be cut back to the nearest node and any side growth cut back to a node as in summer.

The desired shape should grow along the structure, as horizontal growth produces the maximum flowering. Remove any deadwood during the summer when it is easy to detect.

Propagation

From seed or selected cultivars from hardwood cuttings taken in winter.

Opposite: The very beautiful *Liriodendron tulipera* 'Aureomar-ginata'. Crown-raise this tree to a height of 15–20 ft. (4.5–6 m) by removing branches back to collars.

Table: General pruning requirements

KEY:

L   Prune lightly: cut back to node past flowers or remove tips.

M   Prune moderately: cut back up to one-third to a node.

H   Prune hard: cut back one-half or more into old woody growth or near the ground.

3 Ds   Removal of dead, diseased and damaged wood is usually all that is needed, although comments may suggest other pruning, such as crown-thinning. Note that all plants mentioned should have the 3 Ds removed as a matter of course.

Ψ   Use an arborist if pruning involves climbing the tree.

Name	Type	Time	Comments
Abelia	M	After flowering	Can train as hedge.
Abies Ψ	3 Ds	Any time	Can prune damaged leaders.
Acacia Ψ	3 Ds	Any time	Keep shape. Can crown-raise.
Acer Ψ	3 Ds	Summer–early winter	Little pruning needed.
Actinidia	M	Early winter	Thin in summer. Prune old shoots back in winter.
Aesculus Ψ	3 Ds	Any time	Can crown-raise. Prune to maintain a central leader.
Agathis Ψ		Any time	Little pruning required.
Agonis flexuosa Ψ	3 Ds	Any time	Can crown-raise.
Agonis juniperina	L	After flowering	Cut back one-third.
Ailanthus Ψ	3 Ds, H	Any time	Can cut to ground to control growth.
Akebia	L, H	Fall	Can cut to ground each year in milder climates.
Alnus Ψ	3 Ds	Any time	Can crown-raise.
Amelanchier Ψ	3 Ds	Any time	Can cut back old stems in *A. candensis*.
Araucaria Ψ	3 Ds	Any time	Allow room to grow. Can crown-raise or thin whorls.
Arbutus Ψ	3 Ds	Any time	
Banksia Ψ	L	After flowering	Little needed other than shaping.
Berberis	M	After fruiting	Cut back one-half. Can train as hedge.
Betula Ψ	3 Ds	Summer–late winter	Can crown-raise.
Boronia	M	After flowering	Cut back about one-half to keep bushy.
Brachyscome	M	After flowering	Keep compact.
Buddleja alternifolia	M	After flowering	Cut back to new growth.
Buddleja davidii	H	After flowering	Cut back to 12 in. (30 cm).
Buddleja globosa	M	Early spring	Remove weak growth.
Buxus (shrub)	3 Ds	Any time	
Buxus (hedge)	L	Summer	Trim regularly to maintain shape.
Calliandra	L	After flowering	Maintain bushiness.
Callicarpa	L	After flowering	Older plants can be cut back hard.
Callistemon	M	After flowering	Keep compact.
Calluna	M	After flowering	Cut back one-half.
Camellia	M	After flowering	Train sasanquas as hedge, keep shrubs open.
Campsis	M	Spring	Cut back laterals.
Carpinus Ψ	3 Ds	Any time except late winter–early spring	Can crown-raise.

Name	Type	Time	Comments
Ceanothus	H	Summer	Cut back one-half.
Cedrus Ψ	3 Ds	Any time	Keep to one leader.
Cercis Ψ	3 Ds	Any time	
Chaenomeles	L	After flowering	Can train as espalier.
Chamaecyparis Ψ	3 Ds	Any time	
Chimonanthus	L	After flowering	Old plants can be cut back hard.
Choisya	L	After flowering	Keep shaped.
Cistus	L	After flowering	Keep compact.
Citrus	3 Ds	Any time	Cut back to node when picking fruit.
Clematis (early)	L	After flowering	Need little pruning.
Clematis (late)	H	Late winter–early spring	Cut back vines to within 6–12 in. (15–30 cm) of ground.
Clethra	3 Ds	Any time	Remove suckers on *C. alnifolia*.
Coleonema	L	After flowering	Keep compact.
Coprosma	L	Any time	Prune to shape.
Cordyline Ψ		Any time	No pruning except removal of old leaves.
Cornus Ψ	3 Ds	Any time	*C. alba* pruned heavily in spring.
Corylopsis	3 Ds	Any time	Maintain good shape.
Corylus Ψ	3 Ds	Any time	Remove suckers.
Corylus avellana	H	Winter	Prune to ground each year.
Cotinus (foliage)	H	Winter	Hard prune for foliage.
Cotinus (flowers)	L	Any time	Encourages flowering.
Cotoneaster	3 Ds	Any time	Can train as a hedge.
Crataegus	3 Ds	Any time	Old plants can be cut to ground. Can use as hedge.
Crinodendron	3 Ds	Any time	Can crown-raise.
Cryptomeria Ψ	3 Ds	Any time	Can remove lower branches if snow/heavy rain a problem.
Cupressus Ψ	3 Ds	Any time	*C. sempervirens* cultivars can get branch fallout.
Cytisus (shrub)	L	After flowering	Maintain bushiness.
Cytisus	3 Ds	Any time	Little pruning needed.
Daphne	L	After flowering	Cut back to keep shape.
Davidia Ψ	3 Ds	Any time	Little pruning needed.
Desfontainea	3 Ds	Any time	Wear gloves when pruning.
Deutzia	L, H	After flowering	Cut back flowered shoots on old plants.
Diospyros Ψ	3 Ds	Any time	Can crown-raise.
Dodonaea	L	Any time	Can train as hedge.
Drimys Ψ	3 Ds	Any time	
Embothrium	3 Ds	Any time	Little pruning required.
Erica (summer)	L	Spring	Lightly prune.
Erica (winter)	L	After flowering	Lightly prune.
Eriobotrya	L	After fruiting	Older wood can be cut back.
Eriostemon	L	After flowering	Encourages denser growth.
Erythina 'Blakei'	H	After frosts	Cut back to ground.
Erythina	L	After flowering	Cut back old flower stalks.
Escallonia	L	After flowering	Can train as hedge. Old plants can be cut to ground.
Eucalpytus Ψ	3 Ds	Any time	Allow for size.
Euphorbia	H	After flowering	Cut old stems back to ground, or past bracts.
Euryops	M	After flowering	Keep compact.
Fagus Ψ	3 Ds	Any time	Can train as a hedge.
Feijoa	M	After fruiting	Can be trained as hedge.

Name	Type	Time	Comments
Felicia	M	After flowering	Head back/deadhead.
Ficus pumila	L	Any time	Prune to keep juvenile growth.
Forsythia	M	Late spring	Remove old stems. Cut back newer stems lightly.
Fraxinus Ψ	3 Ds	Any time	Allow room to grow. Crown-raise.
Fremontodendron Ψ	3 Ds	Any time	Can reduce top growth.
Fuchsia	L–M	After flowering	Prune tips while growing, cut back after flowering.
Gardenia	L	After flowering	Keep compact.
Garrya	3 Ds	After flowering	Remove spindly growth.
Gaultheria	3 Ds	Any time	Prune to shape.
Gaura	H	After flowering	Cut to ground.
Gelsemium	L	After flowering	Keep compact.
Ginkgo Ψ	3 Ds	Any time	Keep single leader.
Gleditsia Ψ	3 Ds	Any time	Crown-raise if needed. Use gloves.
Gordonia	3 Ds	Any time	Little pruning needed.
Griselinia Ψ	3 Ds	Any time	Can crown-raise.
Hakea	L	After flowering	Keep compact. Can't prune into old wood.
Halesia Ψ	L	After flowering	H. carolina can be pruned to keep compact.
Hamamelis	L	After flowering	Keep compact.
Hardenbergia	H	After flowering	Cut back every second year to ground.
Hebe	L	After flowering	Encourages bushiness and flowering.
Hedera	M–H	Any time	Keep contained.
Heliotropium	M	Early spring	Cut back one-half.
Hibiscus	M	After flowering	Shape. Cut back old plants hard.
Hoheria Ψ	L	Any time	Prune to shape and size.
Hydrangea	M–H	Late summer	Cut back flowering stems to node with 2 buds.
Hypericum	H	Every 2–3 years	Cut hard. Will regenerate well.
Idesia Ψ	3 Ds	Any time	Can crown-raise.
Ilex Ψ	3 Ds	Any time	Can be trained as hedge.
Jacaranda Ψ	3 Ds	Any time	Crown-raise.
Jasminum	M	After flowering	Train to keep shape.
Juglans Ψ	3 Ds	Any time except late winter-early spring.	Can crown-raise. Replace damaged leaders.
Juniperus	L	Any time	Little pruning other than shaping.
Kalmia	3 Ds	Any time	Can remove spent flowers.
Kerria	H	After flowering	Cut back stems older than 2 years.
Kniphofia	3 Ds	Late fall	Remove old flower stalks and leaves to base.
Kolkwitzia	L	After flowering	Thin old flower stems.
Kunzea	L	After flowering	Keep compact.
Laburnum	3 Ds	Any time	Crown-raise. Can create archway.
Lagerstroemia	L	After flowering	Cut back past flowers and prune to shape.
Larix Ψ	3 Ds	Any time	Tree is self-pruning.
Laurus Ψ	3 Ds, L	Any time	Can train as hedge or standard.
Lavandula	M	After flowering	Keep compact.
Lavatera	L	After flowering	Cut back past flowers.
Leonotis	M	After flowering	Keep compact.
Leptospermum	L	After flowering	Keep shaped.
Leucadendron	L	After flowering	Regular light pruning. Prune while cutting flowers.
Leucothoe	H	Fall-early spring	Cut back old flowering stems.

Name	Type	Time	Comments
Liquidambar Ψ	3 Ds	Any time	Can crown-raise. Can fail due to included bark.
Liriodendron Ψ	3 Ds	Any time	Can crown-raise and remove rival leaders. Can fail structurally due to included bark.
Lithodora	L	After flowering	Keep compact.
Lonicera	L	Summer	Trim regularly for hedge.
Loropetalum	L	After flowering	Can train as espalier.
Luculia	L	After flowering	Old stems can be cut back to base.
Magnolia Ψ	3 Ds	Any time	Can crown-raise.
Mahonia	3 Ds, H	Any time	Old stems can be cut to ground.
Malus	L, 3 Ds	Winter	Little pruning needed once frame established.
Maytenus Ψ	3 Ds	Any time	Can remove competing leaders.
Melia Ψ	3 Ds	Any time	Can crown-raise.
Metasequoia Ψ	3 Ds	Any time	Remove competing leaders.
Michelia Ψ	3 Ds	Any time	Can crown-raise.
Morus Ψ	3 Ds	Any time	Little pruning needed.
Myrtus	L	Any time	Can train as hedge.
Nandina	3 Ds, H	Any time	Old stems can be cut to ground.
Nothofagus Ψ	3 Ds	Any time	Try to keep one leader.
Nyssa Ψ	3 Ds	Any time	Train single leader. Can crown-raise.
Olea	3 Ds	Fall-spring	Thin out in fall, cut back winter damage in spring.
Olearia	3 Ds	Any time	Can train as hedge.
Osmanthus	L	Any time	Maintain bushiness.
Paeonia (tree)	3 Ds	Early spring	Cut back past old flowers.
Parthenocissus	L	Fall–winter	Remove unwanted growth.
Paulownia Ψ	L	Summer	Crown-raise.
Pentstemon	L	Summer	Deadhead.
Perovksia	H	Early spring	Cut back to base.
Persea	3 Ds	Any time	Can crown-raise.
Philadelphus	L, H	Summer	Little pruning needed. Cut back older wood.
Phoenix Ψ		Any time	Removal of fronds. Watch spines.
Phormium	L	Any time	Cut back leaves to base if needed. Can divide plant.
Photinia Ψ	M, 3 Ds	Any time	Train as hedge or shrub.
Picea Ψ	3 Ds	Any time	Prune to suitable branch if central leader gets damaged.
Pieris	3 Ds	After flowering	Can be reduced in size.
Pinus Ψ	3 Ds	Any time	Allow room to grow.
Pittosporum Ψ	3 Ds	Any time	Train as hedge or shrub.
Platanus Ψ	3 Ds	Any time	Crown-raise. Can be pollarded.
Plumbago	L	After flowering	Train to desired shape.
Podocarpus Ψ	3 Ds	Any time	Can crown-raise.
Populus Ψ	3 Ds	Any time	Little pruning needed.
Protea	L	After flowering	Keep compact. Prune when cutting flowers.
Prunus (ornamental peach)	3 Ds	Summer–fall	Shape.
Prunus (fruiting peach)	M	Summer–fall	Cut back fruited laterals and thin out other laterals.
Prunus (Japanese plum)	M	After fruiting	Thin old spurs and laterals.
Prunus (European plum)		After fruiting	Remove old spurs.
Prunus (ornamental apricot)	3 Ds	Summer–fall	Maintain shape.
Prunus (fruiting apricot)	M, L	Summer–fall	Thin spurs and laterals.
Prunus (ornamental cherry)	3 Ds	Summer–fall	Shape tree.

Name	Type	Time	Comments
Prunus (fruiting cherry)	3 Ds, L	Summer–fall	Shape, reduce crown.
Prunus (nectarine)	M	Summer–fall	Thin out laterals.
Pseudopanax Ψ	3 Ds	Any time	Needs little pruning.
Psidium	3 Ds	Any time	Remove spindly growth and suckers.
Punica	L	Summer	Tip prune to keep compact.
Pyracantha	L	After flowering	Light pruning to keep shape and encourage berries.
Pyrus	L	After fruiting	Encourage framework, then thin out spurs.
Quercus Ψ	3 Ds	Any time	Develop a single leader. Crown-raise.
Raphiolepis	L	Any time	Little pruning needed.
Rhododendron azalea	L	After flowering	Keep compact. Prune tips.
Rhododendron	L–M	After flowering	Keep compact. Deadhead old flowers. Cut back older plants.
Ribes (blackcurrant)	H	After fruiting	Remove fruited shoots.
Ribes (red and white currant)	L	Late winter–early spring.	Remove old and weak growth
Ribes (gooseberry)	M	Winter	Cut back one-half for first 2 years.
Robinia Ψ	3 Ds	Any time	Crown-raise. Use gloves.
Rosa	M–H	After flowering and frosts	Prune hard to encourage new growth and flowers.
Rosmarinus	L	After flowering	Trim to keep compact or train as hedge.
Rubus (fall)	H	Late winter–early spring	Cut canes to ground level.
Rubus (summer)	H	Winter, fall	Tie canes in winter. Cut fruited canes to ground in fall.
Rubus (blackberry, raspberry)	H	After fruiting	Remove old canes, tie in new ones.
Ruscus	3 Ds	Spring	Cut back spindly growth. Use gloves.
Salix Ψ	3 Ds	Any time	Allow room to grow.
Salvia	L	After flowering	Cut back one-third.
Santolina	H	After flowering	Cut back to base. Deadhead in fall.
Sarcococca	3 Ds	Any time	Little pruning.
Schinus Ψ	3 Ds	Any time	Can crown-raise.
Sequoia Ψ	3 Ds	Any time	Remove suckers at base.
Skimmia	3 Ds	Any time	Little pruning needed.
Sophora Ψ	3 Ds	Any time	Little pruning needed.
Sorbus Ψ	3 Ds	Any time	Can crown-raise. Form a good leader.
Spiraea (previous year)	L	After flowering	Light pruning.
Spiraea (current growth)	H	After flowering	Cut to within 4 in. (10 cm) of ground.
Stachyurus	3 Ds	After flowering	Cut back spindly stems.
Stenocarpus	3 Ds	Any time	Crown-raise or prune to size.
Stewartia	3 Ds	Any time	Can crown-raise.
Styrax	3 Ds	Any time	Crown-raise.
Symphoricarpos	3 Ds	Late winter	Remove suckers from *S. alba*. Remove weak growth.
Syringa	L, H	After flowering	Lightly prune. Cut back old plants hard.
Tamarix (early spring)	L	Late spring	Remove one-third of growth.
Tamarix (summer)	H	Winter	Cut to within 12 in. (30 cm) of ground.
Taxodium Ψ	3 Ds	Any time	Little pruning needed.
Taxus Ψ	3 Ds	Any time	Prune to keep shape.
Telopea	L	After flowering	Prune to encourage bushiness and flowering.
Teucrium	L	Any time	Regular trimming to keep compact.
Thryptomeme	L	After flowering	Cut back past flowers.
Thuja Ψ	3 Ds	Any time	Can reduce length of branches if under snow.
Thymus	L	After flowering	Cut back past flowers.
Tilia Ψ	3 Ds	Summer	Single leader preferred. Can pleach.

Name	Type	Time	Comments
Toona	3 Ds	Any time	Reduce crown. Remove suckers.
Trachelospermum	L	Fall	Cut back weak growth arising from main growth.
Tsuga Ψ	3 Ds	Any time	Little pruning needed.
Ulmus Ψ	3 Ds	Any time	Crown-thin and remove suckers.
Umbellularia Ψ	3 Ds	Any time	Little pruning needed.
Vaccinium	3 Ds	Spring	Remove weak growth.
Viburnum	L	After flowering	Keep compact.
Virgilia Ψ	3 Ds	Any time	Can crown-raise.
Vitis	L	Early winter	Establish strong arms, cut back strong laterals to 2 buds.
Weigelia	M, H	Summer	Older stems can be cut back hard.
Wisteria	L	Winter	Keep compact.

Glossary

Apical bud The bud at the tip of the stem, also known as a terminal bud.

Arm A branch arising from the main stem of a grape.

Branch A limb or shoot arising from the trunk of the tree.

Branch collar Trunk tissue that forms around the base of a branch between the main stem and the branch. Provides a protective zone as well as strength for branch.

Bud A condensed shoot that may contain leaves or flowers. Flower buds are usually fatter than leaf buds.

Callus Tissue that forms over any wound made on a woody plant.

Co-dominant stems Stems or trunks of about the same size originating from the same position from the main stem. When the stem bark ridge turns upward the union is strong; when the ridge turns inward the union is weak.

Compartmentalization Tree defense process that enables a tree to resist the spread of disease-causing organisms.

Coppicing Cutting back trees and shrubs hard to produce timber or foliage.

Crotch The junction of primary branches with the trunk of the tree. Trees with narrow crotch angles are more likely to break.

Crown Portion of tree consisting of branches and leaves and any part of the trunk from which branches arise.

Crown-cleaning The removal of the 3 Ds: dead, diseased or damaged wood.

Crown-raising The removal of the lower branches to give better ground clearance.

Crown-reduction The reduction of the height and spread of a tree.

Crown-thinning Removal of weak, spindly growth and criss-crossing branches.

Deadheading Removal of spent flowers or fruit from a plant.

Deciduous Seasonal shedding of plant parts, usually leaves.

Dormant Growth is suspended.

Epicormic shoots Shoots produced by dormant buds within the bark or stems of a tree as a result of stress or topping.

Espalier A plant trained flat against a wall or fixed in horizontal layers to a climbing structure.

Evergreen Plants that retain their foliage.

Framework Basic structure of trunk, stem and main branches.

Hardwood stem cutting A stem cutting taken from wood of the previous season's growth.

Heading back Cutting the end shoots back to a node. This encourages bushiness and flowering.

Included bark Inwardly formed bark at the junction of branches or co-dominant stems. This union is inherently weak.

Lateral A side-growth of any kind on a shrub or tree.

Lopping See topping.

Leader The shoot that ends a branch and grows in the same direction. Generally one strong leader is retained.

Node A point on the stem where a new shoot will arise from a bud.

Pleaching A method of training trees to form a hedge at the same height, keeping the lower trunk bare.

Pollarding Cutting back a tree to a well-defined framework each year.

Scarification A method of weakening the covering of hard case seeds to hasten germination.

Semi-ripe stem cutting A stem cutting taken from growth that has hardened off.

Softwood stem cutting A stem cutting taken from soft, immature growth.

Spur A short branch system that carries clusters of flower heads.

Stratification A method of treating dormant seeds by chilling under moist conditions to effect germination.

Target pruning The final cut when removing branches, the cut being as close as possible to the branch collar.

Tip prune Removing the growing tip back to a node.

Topiary Specialized pruning of plants into specific shapes.

Topping Indiscriminate cutting of branches.

Bibliography

Australian Standard: Pruning of Amenity Trees.

Bryant, Geoff. *Gardens for Free*. David Bateman, 1992.

Harrison, Richmond. *Handbook of Trees and Shrubs*. A.H. & A.W. Reed, 1974.

Malins, John. *The Pruner's Handbook*. David & Charles, 1992.

Metcalf, Laurie. *The Cultivation of New Zealand Trees and Shrubs*. A.H. & A.W. Reed, 1972.

Palmer, Stanley. *Palmers Manual of Trees, Shrubs and Climbers*. Lancewood Publishing, 1994.

Shigo, Alex. *A New Tree Biology*. Durham, 1986.

Index

160